HIDDEN TRUTHS

HIDDEN TRUTHS

WHAT LEADERS NEED TO HEAR BUT ARE RARELY TOLD

David Fubini

WILEY

Published by John Wiley & Sons, Inc., Hoboken, New Jersey.
Published simultaneously in Canada.

For general information on our other products and services or for technical support, please contact our Customer Care Department within the United States at (800) 762–2974, outside the United States at (317) 572–3993, or fax (317) 572–4002.

Wiley publishes in a variety of print and electronic formats and by print-on-demand. Some material included with standard print versions of this book may not be included in e-books or in print-on-demand. If this book refers to media such as a CD or DVD that is not included in the version you purchased, you may download this material at http://booksupport.wiley.com. For more information about Wiley products, visit www.wiley.com.

Library of Congress Cataloging-in-Publication Data is available:

ISBN 9781119682332 (Hardcover)
ISBN 9781119682356 (ePDF)
ISBN 9781119682349 (ePub)

Cover Design: Paul McCarthy
Cover Art: © Getty Images | Miragec

Printed in the United States of America.

SKY10021792_101620

For my wife Bertha and our four wonderful children:
Michael, William, Anna, and Marco

Contents

This book is divided into 15 chapters that, collectively, delineate important learning that all new CEOs and leaders must understand. The title of each chapter completes the following sentences.

New CEOs must learn how to:

Foreword

As the leader of two companies—Danaher and General Electric—I've learned the hidden truths about being a CEO the hard way. David Fubini makes it easier for future leaders and CEOs.

In between these two stints as CEO, I taught at the Harvard Business School, which is where I got to know David. We co-taught the introductory courses on Organizational Behavior and Leadership. We also joined to teach second-year students about the challenge of executing strategy and we have taught executives together. I also learned my own truth about David: He understands CEOs; he also understands the reality of the job and what happens behind the curtain of the CEO role.

I'll admit, I have a certain wariness when it comes to management consultants. I think it is critical for an organization to build their own capabilities and develop their own insights to be able to address important topics. Yet, the value of a third-party, impartial view, informed by the best practice of others can be enlightening and helpful. Such is the case with David's three decades experience as a management consultant at McKinsey, providing an invaluable source for insights for new leaders. David has torn the veneer off the role of CEO to let others see the reality of the difficult trade-offs, the challenges of day-to-day management, and the highs and lows of the job in a manner that is illuminating and beneficial to other CEOs and leaders. In this way, it is not a traditional management consultant's perspective. This is a more personal counselor's view of the challenges of being a chosen CEO or leader.

David's belief that few people really grasp what this top leadership job entails is right on the mark. His conviction that knowing the 14 hidden truths can be a huge help to leaders is equally valid.

I know this because I've walked it—and I wish I had these 14 truths in hand from the start.

At Danaher, a global science and technology company, I established a decentralized leadership style, focused much of our efforts on hiring and training, and implemented a series of measures that helped Danaher achieve a great deal of success. Although I was prepared for a lot of what leading this company involved, I discovered that the moment I assumed the CEO role, the clock was ticking—loudly. The board wanted to be sure that they had made the right choice for the job. Wall Street analysts were eagerly watching to see what changes we'd make. Employees, suppliers, and other stakeholders were observing and analyzing my every move.

David emphasizes the need to arrive prepared—this was a truth that hit home during those initial weeks and months on the job.

His observation about being cautious about becoming isolated from the rest of the organization is important. CEOs are faced with many big decisions with huge ramifications, and there are few who share in the consequences of the results of those actions. That can be isolating and somewhat difficult to get your mind around until it actually happens. I sought to counter this challenge by building a team around me to get diverse viewpoints and a range of perspectives. I learned the value of seeking out truth tellers, creating a culture where you encourage putting both the good and the bad on the table.

You can't do this from the CEO's desk; you have to travel a lot, meet directly with those closest to your customers, and talk with outsiders, not just insiders. As I'm fond of saying, there's a huge benefit from "not eating off the same menu." This approach was one of the hallmarks of my time at Danaher and what we are underway building at GE.

CEOs often don't know what they're getting into, even when they know a great deal about the businesses that they're hired to lead. At GE, I was on the board prior to my colleagues turning to me and asking if I would consider taking the job as chairman and CEO. David reminded me that when we were teaching at Harvard, a student asked why I accepted when I could have just rested on my laurels earned at Danaher. I told the student I was too young not to want the challenge of another leadership role and, perhaps more importantly, that I relished both the challenge and the opportunity to save an iconic American company—one that was started by Thomas Edison.

You work hard to be prepared for a new leadership role and yet it's only when you get in the ring that you really know the full scope of the fight. No one really understands the full nuance of the situation—the inevitable constraints on time to act, talent you have inherited, and capital, which never seems enough. I've always believed that organizations must continuously work to improve and drive change, but changing in the midst of a crisis such as the one GE has gone through is something else entirely. There's the expression "Changing the tires on a moving truck" that is applicable. David writes about the importance of "changing the management as a critical step in making change happen," and I've had to grapple with a lot of these changes in talent in my top team. It's never easy, but it's necessary.

I also found David's discussion of boards enlightening and aligned with my own experiences. Having served on a number of boards in different industries, including GE, T. Rowe Price, and GlaxoSmithKline, I know how challenging it can be for first-time CEOs to deal with this new type of oversight. Boards can be quick to provide perspectives and critiques despite the fact they meet roughly six to ten times during the course of a year. Plus, new CEOs must navigate the transition from having one boss to now having many. Using baseball as an analogy, as I have been both a player and an owner, I can tell you with certainty a 90-mile fastball sure seems a lot faster when you're in the batter's box than when you are in the owner's box.

At the same time, I agree with David that if CEOs establish true partnerships with boards, it can be an incredibly valuable relationship. Why? Because of their combined diverse experience and wisdom, their networks of valuable experts, and their willingness to provide honest feedback that may not be available from anyone else.

And yes, humility matters—a lot. Leaders need to remember, it's not about you. One of my first actions at Danaher was to start the discussion about my eventual successor. The board was surprised—"Hey, we just promoted you"—but this is a crucial CEO task for the enterprise's continued success. David correctly notes how important this responsibility is for CEOs, as well as knowing the right time to depart. I left Danaher when the company was doing well and the board had multiple succession candidates. I assessed it was time for the organization to continue to change—for new leadership with a fresh view. I didn't have to leave, but I knew it was time.

When David and I were teaching together at Harvard, we'd inform a class about something that appeared to us to be an obvious managerial truism about leadership. We'd later ask each other, "Wouldn't students have known this?" But they didn't. Similarly, I learned not to assume that because I know something about being a CEO, others would know it as well.

And that's the beauty of this book. It's the ultimate inside baseball look at being a CEO. What David knows about this challenging, fascinating, and at times frustrating job, most people don't. Until you read this terrific book. Then you'll know the truths.

Larry Culp

Preface

As a consultant at McKinsey & Co. for nearly 35 years, I have helped CEOs navigate some of the most difficult transitions and other challenges they face on the job. These decisions centered on critical issues such as: selling part of their own company or merging with another one; drastically reorganizing the whole organization, making a massive strategic shift in the marketplace, and dealing with the demands of consumers, boards, and shareholders; and navigating the non-market forces shaped by government, demographics, and cultural trends. All of these situations are enormously complicated, and the stakes are always high. Corporate legacy, jobs, revenues, investments, careers, personal reputations, and shareholder value are on the line. While the rewards of running a company are great, the risks of the job are sometimes even greater. After those 35 years, I came away convinced of this truth: Being a CEO is a singularly tough job, and to be successful, these leaders need help to know not only about basic leadership principles but also the "hidden truths" that are part of the role's daily challenges. Too often, these truths are the difference between success and failure.

Since retiring as a senior partner at McKinsey to teach at Harvard Business School, I've become familiar with the advice offered in business books and articles to help leaders. I must admit that many of these works have left me a bit disappointed. While their authors offer interesting insights, they do so from a vantage point that doesn't seem to reflect the reality and practical aspects of CEOs' daily lives—lives that I observed firsthand. I was acutely aware of these aspects—the multiple agendas of senior staff, the unknowns imbedded in many situations, the variety and conflicting desires of various stakeholders, the intense stress of the job—and they were often missing from books, articles, and former CEOs' lofty speeches. Their authors frequently wrote as if leaders (or leadership problems) existed within an ideal business state, where problems were analyzed dispassionately and solutions ensued logically.

Here's another crucial truth that these authors miss about the challenges business leaders continually face: CEOs and their executive teams, no matter how accomplished, have very human reactions to being in high-stakes situations. When that human nature is put under consistent pressure in a context that demands clear and quick decision-making, poor processes and bad habits often result. I've witnessed countless situations in which very smart business people made awful decisions because of the emotional, interpersonal, and communications messes they've managed to make.

Hidden Truths: What leaders need to hear but are rarely told offers approaches and frameworks to deal effectively with the real business world of human beings under pressure. It assumes that CEOs have weaknesses and foibles common to all of us while also understanding that the situations CEOs face are uncommon and extraordinary. Indeed, as of this writing, we are in the midst of a worldwide pandemic and a new social dialogue in the US around racial disparity, which has generated a range of uncommon and extraordinary issues that are posing daunting challenges to CEOs. No doubt, more such issues will arise in the coming months and years.

As the title of the book suggests, CEOs are often surprised by the stark reality of their roles—surprised in their initial weeks and months on the job as well as years later. CEOs may enter the job with high expectations, but they often become overwhelmed by new circumstances, finding themselves surprisingly isolated from the rest of the organization and learning that the data and information delivered from senior leadership often lacks clarity or transparency—or both. Many CEOs also struggle to initiate organizational changes. This struggle can occur in a recently inherited organization where their often-complicated relationship with a new board increases these transition challenges. It can also occur when CEOs have been on the job for a sustained period of time and they grapple with a rapidly evolving competitive landscape, a more engaged board, and an entrenched culture at odds with new strategic direction.

Through the many case studies and stories included in this book, readers will see the wide variety of problems that arise when CEOs *don't* take care to hear the truth and *don't* embrace the reality of their new roles. Too often new CEOs think the scholarly articles and frameworks and flow charts that business and academic texts outline are what they need to master. The realty is far more challenging.

In writing this book, I'm forcing myself to relive some of the difficult situations I saw during my career and assess what took place—the mistakes made, the mistakes that might have been avoided—with the benefit of hindsight. Without the restrictions inherent in the consultant-client relationship, I can assess with complete freedom. But far more importantly, writing a book creates some distance from *the heat of the moment* (for me and for CEOs and leaders reading this), when emotions run high and reason is sometimes in short supply. Using that distance, I hope to improve the performance of current and future leaders by providing helpful perspectives, processes, and mindsets that can be employed *before* their leadership is (almost inevitably) pushed to a crisis moment.

Just because I am freed from consultant-client restrictions doesn't mean I'm able to name every name in the examples mentioned in this book. I will identify CEOs and other leaders when they've given me permission to do so, or their stories are a matter of public record, or when they have appeared as part of Harvard Business School case studies. I have also relied on my own personal interactions with some clients that I do name as they are in the somewhat distant past but whose lessons remain relevant to today's challenges. In some instances, however, I will disguise identities because of the sensitivity of the material.

This book is particularly focused on CEOs because these leaders face situations that are particular to the office. Keep in mind that when people become CEOs, they face two transitions at once: dealing with their own personal adjustments to a very new role, while simultaneously helping the organizations they run adjust to new leadership. This is especially daunting for first-time CEOs, even if they have enjoyed enormous success in other executive positions. The CEO occupies a role that is like no other in a company, making the stakes, the responsibilities, and even the mechanics of decision-making truly novel. The highly distinctive nature of the job can be challenging not only during the early part of their tenure, but also for years afterward.

Today, most CEOs need to be aware of the realities of the job. They need resources that address issues that are complex and confusing and for which their previous positions haven't prepared them. They need the insights of CEOs who have gone before them, who speak honestly and sometimes provocatively about the challenges they met—and in some instances, didn't meet. I hope this book can, at least in part, satisfy these needs.

Acknowledgments

Many people helped to make this book a reality, and I am grateful for their assistance.

I want to thank Larry Culp, not only for taking the time to write a Foreword for this book, but also for his colleagueship and friendship, both while he was at Harvard Business School and now in his new role as the CEO of GE. Larry's humility, his brilliance as a leader, and his commitment to excellence in all that he does is a wonderful reminder of what true leadership looks like.

I also want to thank my Harvard Business School faculty colleagues for embracing me and teaching me to be a better thought leader and educator than anyone would have expected when I joined HBS five years ago. I joined the faculty in order to remain close to the leading edge of business thought and to continue to learn and evolve as a business leader. Every day, I am blessed to be learning from and being challenged by this group of extraordinary educators, academics, and professionals all—the while having the wonderful opportunity to help educate the next generation of business leaders. In particular, I want to thank Dean Nitin

Nohria for his mentorship, coaching, and friendship, over the more than a decade that I've known him.

None of the hidden truths in this book would've seen the light of day without my McKinsey & Co. colleagues. Over my 35-year career, I learned from, was guided by, and worked collaboratively with a vast array of professional colleagues who were brilliant counselors to clients. McKinsey is a unique institution with a wonderful professional commitment to client service and a relentless commitment to advancing managerial learning. I have been the direct beneficiary of this professional commitment, and in my time there, I gained insights about CEOs and other leaders that provided the original inspiration for this book.

I'm often asked by my students, What do I miss most about my former career at McKinsey? While I miss my former colleagues, I miss my clients at least as much. I loved being a counselor and advisor. Thank you to the many clients who allowed me to hone my craft. I provided them with advice and counsel that I hope furthered their goals and aspirations, and they provided me with a true understanding of what great leadership entails. Across the hundreds of clients that I served, it is hard to single out any one individual, but I should say that I would not have been able to have the career I had without Claude "Bud" Moore from General Motors. In the five years that Bud and I worked together, I learned from him how to be a "true" client counselor. Bud's humility, commitment to others, and unwavering focus on the institution that he loved inspired me then as it does now.

I also want to acknowledge the incredible efforts of Bill Fallon, Purvi Patel, and the rest of the Wiley team who have been so helpful in guiding the publication of this book. Similarly, I want to thank Bruce Wexler for his support and for his outstanding editing and general insights.

1

Arrive Prepared

Every day as new CEO is a rude awakening. Just-arrived leaders of an organization, in a role that they have aspired to and worked diligently for years to achieve, soon face the stark reality that the highly developed skills that positioned them for this leadership role are of little value to their organizational success. From the first few weeks in the role to five years down the line, the demands of the position are vastly different from the operational leadership skills that produced the record of achievement allowing for advancement to a CEO role. This is surprising and, for many, shocking—given the complexity that comes with being a modern-day CEO.

This harsh reality is even more pronounced since the most immediate challenge for all new CEOs, be they outsiders or promoted insiders, is to arrive prepared.

The CEO's job has become exceedingly more challenging than even in the recent past. Many CEOs don't realize how they must prepare themselves for the challenge ahead. The intensity of the leadership challenge, the tsunami of issues and constituents to be addressed, and the limited time and high expectations for immediate results are rarely fully anticipated by new leaders. While they may be aware of the strategic challenge, few anticipate the talent deficits, the competitive market demands, legal nightmares, regulatory gauntlets, and financial conundrums that are integral to the position.

In today's market environment, the CEO's job isn't as simple as leading an organization to deliver a return to shareholders exceeding the cost of capital. Now CEOs must address a vast array of confounding issues, balancing many managerial trade-offs: time (to act), talent (to execute), and capital (to finance). New CEOs are expected to be able to respond immediately to a vast number of wide-ranging questions that include:

- How do you plan to deliver short-term results without sacrificing long-term sustainability?
- Does your existing organization have the right structure, systems, and talent to deliver these results?
- Is your balance sheet and capital structure sufficient to fund the programs you anticipate needing to launch?
- What do you want to say to the vast array of customers who want to know what you plan to change and how quickly you're going to change the products and services that affect their businesses and interests?
- How well positioned are you within your community and with the political leaders that all believe they have a stake in the decisions that you are about to make?
- How do you plan to position your diverse company to analysts who want to categorize your company into neat segments that align with their predetermined positions of value, growth, and so forth?
- How do you respond to viral social media posts and Twitter traffic that have an uninformed, yet publicly influential impact on internal and external company audiences?
- How do you generate cash flow to fund operations but not attract activists whose models track cash as an early indication of a value play?

- How do you ensure compliance with the vast array of regulatory agencies all dictating ever-increasing numbers of demands?
- How can you remain socially conscious, given that it seems like little time, money, or energy remains for necessary causes?
- How do you keep your board of directors happy and meet the expectations they had in hiring you?

Consider a recently appointed CEO—let's call him Jack. He arrives at his large organization with big plans for his upcoming tenure. Jack has waited his whole career actively planning and positioning himself for this leadership opportunity to arrive. For years, he's thought about what he would do when he was in charge. Jack is eager to put his extensive global management experience to use; he knows the technological innovations and operational moves that he believes will create a quantum leap in performance. Given his extensive experience, Jack is determined to lead others differently and more effectively than the way he has been managed. He is thrilled the board has elected him, and he is anxious to meet their lofty expectations.

What Jack doesn't know, however, is that his new company is heading into a hurricane of issues: within a month of his appointment, a combination of a competitor's breakthrough products, the weakness of his inherited management team, the demands of the multiple constituents seeking his time and attention, and a failed acquisition has attracted an activist investor who is questioning the quality of the company's strategy and the return from its operations. Jack is forced into firefighting mode, scrambling to respond reactively and quickly realizing that he never was able to deliver on his carefully planned series of technical and operation plans.

Jack's story isn't unusual. An unrelenting demand for fast turnarounds, improved performance, and financial results is commonplace. CEOs must grapple with shareholder requirements, a changing, diversifying workforce, employees striving for professional and personal life balance, and the need for community acceptance/service. Rating agencies, buy- and sell-side analysts, the ever-threatening presence of activists, and preying private equity (PE) firms all ratchet up the intensity.

On top of that, CEOs are on the clock. They no longer have the luxury of time, the ability to wait for things to sort themselves out. In a fast-changing environment, seconds count. CEOs need a sharp and clear direction shaped by a vision of the future of the company—and the path to that vision must be taken quickly.

To meet these challenges, CEOs don't just need to arrive; they need to arrive prepared.

A NEW AND DEMANDING ERA

In the past, CEOs had a much different economic climate with more leisurely timeframes to enact change. Boards of directors often hired them mainly because of their demonstrated past talent, not necessarily their detailed future vision. Many new leaders were expected to have a reasonable amount of time—often months—to figure out how the company really worked and to develop a prescription for change and begin enacting major new initiatives. Referred to as a "honeymoon period," this initial timeframe might involve meeting individually with executives, going on road shows to visit facilities, hosting "listening tours" with major channel participants and customers, and generally enjoying a period of reflective thinking. After the honeymoon ended, CEOs could present thoughtful plans and approaches informed by the homework they had done. This is hardly ever the case anymore. Now, traditional timeframes for new CEOs to form a team, diagnose needed changes, and define action plans have been dramatically compressed. In the past, turnarounds necessitated by the previous CEO's failure sometimes required this accelerated approach. Now, even a normal transition of leadership requires decisive and speedy actions.

CEOs are often shocked by this demand for immediate action. If they haven't done their homework or lack a theory in the case that helps them implement change in confusing, complex situations, they may well find themselves unable to act—and in today's environment, inaction is almost always counterproductive and costly to all stakeholders.

In mid-2017, General Electric changed CEOs. After Jeff Immelt's long-planned departure was executed, the board chose John Flanner to be CEO. In an early interview, Flanner let it be known that it would be approximately four months before new strategy shifts and updates to earnings targets would be announced. During an analysts' conference he said his review would take time but said it had not altered GE's 2017 outlook. The market reacted negatively to the news, driving the stock price down 3% in a single day. The *Wall Street Journal* quoted Jeff Windau, an analyst at Edward Jones, as saying, "People want to get the answers sooner." Deane Dray, an analyst at RBC Capital, seemed to concur as he was quoted observing that GE would be "in a state of limbo" until the review was finished. The market abhors any vacuum and so fills it with concern and a sense of downside risk, and a negative cycle can be launched.

More concerning, when the turnaround plan was announced incrementally over time, it called for a radical redefinition of the entire company. The shock to many constituents was profound as few were prepared for the step function nature of the suggested changes. The delay also reinforced the resistance to major change that historically always exists. The new CEO's radical change in tone and expectations shook investors, analysts, and shareholders. Ultimately, Flannery lasted less than a year in the role before being replaced by Larry Culp. Partially as a result, GE dropped from the Dow Jones Index and the company prepared to be broken apart, as whole units divested, major layoffs were enacted, and new management was bought in. A rethinking of the entire corporation structure also took place, including a radical resizing of the corporate headquarters. We'll never know, but if Flanner had arrived better prepared—if he had hit the ground running with these plans finalized and ready to be enacted—the reaction within and outside of GE might have been different.

As difficult as it is for long-tenured CEOs to make fast decisions, it's even harder for those new to the role—and more new CEOs exist than ever before. A recent *Wall Street Journal* article noted that in the first five months of 2017, 13 companies with market values in excess of $40 billion had installed new CEOs—some often quite suddenly. This included such household names as Ford, Caterpillar, Fiat/Chrysler, and AIG. In June of 2017 alone, new CEOs were appointed at GE, Uber, Whirlpool, Buffalo Wild Wings, Perrigo, and Pandora. Of these, only Whirlpool was not facing activist pressure at the time of these management moves.

Why are CEOs under such intense pressure to take quick action? Here are three factors that every CEO should be aware of and prepare themselves for:

1. **The Impatience of Markets and Investors.** Analysts and the broader market were conditioned to allow for a honeymoon period, but the market now demands shorter investment cycles accompanied by actions that are the result of strategic clarity. They want to see forceful personalities prescribing forceful actions. New CEOs have to work in an environment of increased market sophistication, digital transformation, and cutting-edge modeling and simulations; they also have to deal with increased transparency as a result of social media and the multiplicity of global communication forums/exchanges. Boards that used to have a balanced view of the short and long term, are increasingly forced by today's market context to focus less on long-term strategic renewal in favor of more immediate actions.

2. **Emergence of the Private Equity Secondary Market and the Rise of Activism.** PE firms now provide an

attractive secondary market for unwanted assets, and all manner of activists stand ready to act as a check on slow-acting management. Historically, a new CEO might have had to live with a slow wind down or sale to a strategic buyer of underperforming businesses. Now, private equity provides the means for strategic acceleration. The market has come to expect that CEOs will address underperforming businesses and unwanted assets quickly, in part by using PE firms to market and monetize unwanted assets. This secondary market also enables activists and other market influencers to force divestitures and reshape corporate portfolios faster than in the past. Activism has had a profound effect on boards, and boards in turn have pressured CEOs to respond. A new and growing investor class of activism has emerged with a wide continuum of investors ranging from the "radical and confrontational" to those who are "accommodating but insistent." Finally, corporate social responsibility groups bring their own form of activism, motivating boards to meet the needs of these stakeholders and avoid the negative press that might accompany their failure to act forcefully.

3. **Change in Board Attitudes toward CEO Tenure and Selection.** Boards and shareholders have never welcomed failure, but they are far less tolerant of it today than in the past. As a result, boards are much more willing to fire CEOs. Getting rid of a CEO used to be anathema for a board because it was a sign of failure of their governance. Now it may be considered a governance strength, and at the very least, it's a more acceptable board behavior. Similarly, boards are looking to hire stars who have "been there, done that." They want to be able to say, "We hired Julie because she turned around Company X; we knew she had this capability." At the same time, they are increasingly under pressure to question the perceived value of "qualified" internal candidates who have never been CEO.

All this means that CEOs need a different start-up game plan than their predecessors. It's not just that they are pressured to produce excellent results immediately. It's that they need to prepare themselves by obtaining key insights and perspectives before they even accept the position and through the preparatory phase as they come on board to the new job. CEOs must use the interview phase as due diligence on the issues and needed operational changes. Listening carefully and thoughtfully even while interviewing for the role is a critical skill, and one too often ignored in the rush to impress.

Consider how Roger Krone, formerly of Boeing and now CEO of Leidos, made the transition.

ROGER KRONE: DOING YOUR HOMEWORK

In late 2013, Leidos (a large defense/health care company providing software and services to many government and defense agencies) was searching for a new CEO. One of the candidates was Roger Krone, who had risen close to the top at Boeing and who was looking for an opportunity to be a CEO. During this period, the Leidos board was particularly worried about the company's strategy, its recent performance, and the no-longer-remote possibility that the company might be the target for an activist investor. While earnings were acceptable, prospects for future growth were constrained, and yet the business was generating large amounts of cash flow—an enticement to an activist.

To effect a needed turnaround and fend off any unfriendly initiatives from the outside, the board members were eager to find a CEO who could change things quickly. There were three main sets of questions the board asked to make their assessment.

The first set concerned Krone's plans for changing the company in the early days of his tenure. How would he assess the Leidos portfolio? What parts of the company would he retain and what parts of the company would he sell? The board pressed him on his first quarter plans, especially how he would assess the need for financial change and how much cultural change might be needed to attain his financial goals.

The second set of questions concerned the team he would use to execute his plans. The board told Krone: "We're not just hiring you; we're going to be hiring your network." The board wanted to assess Krone's network. The company's senior management team had a short bench (due in large part to the formation of Leidos when it was created as a result of the split of the former company SAIC). As it turned out, Krone had an impressive network, reassuring the board that he could bring needed talent to the senior team.

Third, the board was also concerned about his ability to make the shift from CFO/Business Unit manager to CEO, and a series of questions were posed to assess this ability.

Krone's responses about both his network and his immediate plans demonstrated that he was ready to tackle a challenging position. Krone had obviously spent time studying the company, thinking about these issues, and authoring a preliminary plan for what he would do if he were appointed CEO. He had a point of view about what parts of the company he would sell and the high performers he might recruit to the company. This preparation not only helped him get the job but made it more likely that he possessed the knowledge and resources necessary to be effective immediately.

HOW DID KRONE DEVELOP ALL THESE PERSPECTIVES? HE HAD HELP

Roger had relied on his network of contacts in the defense industry to give him detailed views on the positives and challenges within Leidos. He sought information from the defense department and the intelligence community as to how they viewed Leidos and their sense about the degree of change required by a new CEO. He worked with a friendly, seasoned investment banker deeply familiar with the defense industry who provided all manner of financial models, industry background, and analyst views of the company and its value position with investors. Krone spoke with former board members and suppliers who worked with both Boeing and Leidos. He collaborated closely with the executive search firm that led the search, gaining a deeper understanding of the board, who were its members, and how they thought. He listened carefully to the story of the board's evolving issues (post breakup) and what their decision criteria were likely to be. As a result, Roger arrived with better and deeper insights and a more substantive six-month plan than his chief rival, who was an internal candidate.

HOW DO YOU PREPARE? GO DEEP AND BROAD

Years ago, CEOs arrived in their roles with a "maintenance mentality" for a period of months during which they could learn and understand what was required for change. No more. Today, boards want CEOs who possess the potential to "drive an inflection point on the curve." Translated, this means they need CEOs prepared to recognize required turning points and who can drive change at these points quickly and effectively.

To meet this expectation, CEOs require a deep and broad understanding of the situation they are coming into. Time pressure and board and business environment expectations, however, make the "six month, visit all the sites, and meet all the stakeholders" approach of the past impossible. So new sources of data and insights must be tapped *before arrival into the role*, and this must be done quickly and efficiently.

Obvious and Not So Obvious—"Must Dos"

CEO candidates face two immediate sets of questions as they assess their new role: (1) How to obtain the critical information necessary to evaluate their potential new company? (2) Where to find the resources to help gather and make sense of that information?

One might think these questions apply only to new CEOs who are external hires. Surprisingly, internal candidates are often as ill prepared as their external competitors for these leadership roles. In many cases they may suffer from the "incumbent curse": the inability to look objectively at the situation they may be inheriting. While internal candidates understand the operating culture of their organizations, they are often in denial about the depth of challenges and changes that the business requires. Too often, they overrate the quality of their management team and believe that they possess greater capability for change than they do. Internal candidates may also falsely believe they have a full view of the wide variety of complicated and complex challenges they will inherit. As one internally promoted CEO said to me, "I thought I saw the whole chess board, then I took the top job and realized what I was actually seeing was only a small portion of what turns out to be a three dimensional chess board with fully half of the board hidden from my view."

What Do You Need to Know?

Quality of the Business and the State of Its Existing Operations: Understanding these general challenges is the "must do" for any leadership due diligence. One must have an in-depth understanding of the quality of the strategy and resulting operational and market success of the business. Gaining a sense of the quality of supplier relations and the position of the company with its customers and channels is essential, as is past management's performance in these areas. Assessing the effectiveness of operational structures and management processes are also crucial tasks. To arrive prepared, these prerequisites are starting points, not end points.

What the Board Believes and How It Works. Beyond the hiring process, all your future plans for change will be guided and overseen by the same individuals that just hired you into the CEO role. Much as the Roger Krone example illustrates, the selection process is an important time for learning and assessing your future board and understanding their expectations as well as learning their sense of where the challenges and strengths lie in your new portfolio of inherited businesses.

The interview process should be an evaluation process for both the board and you. You need to use the time together to actively listen not only to the leadership challenge of the company but also to gauge how the board is playing their role. What is the culture of the board? How do members interact with one another? Are there factions, and if so, why? Is the board financially focused or operationally oriented? What is their expected level of involvement? To what degree will it need to be informed and involved?

Experience might suggest that since CEO's changes are usually undertaken when a shift is necessary, boards will welcome change. However, there's no guarantee that the *degree* of change the board wants will agree with the degree of change desired by the CEO, or that the *kind* of change that a new CEO may promise will be compatible with their views. The "degree of openness and acceptance" must be assessed early on. If this assessment isn't done, CEOs may join a company thinking radical change will be welcomed while the board is risk averse and seeks "major shifts but not transformation"—a direct quote from one board member following a failed CEO transition.

So, as a part of the due diligence, you need to understand the board's true desire for change: Questions that will help include:

What is the tenure of each of the board members?

Who brought them onto the board?

What was their "true" relationship with the last CEO, versus what might have been said publicly?

Was it contentious or harmonious?

If contentious, what was it about the past CEO that made it so?

How widely shared was this contentious feeling?

Does the board want slow and steady or fast and disruptive change?

How aligned are they in this belief?

Quality and Experience of Senior Talent Pool. Outstanding teams make outstanding leaders. Given this truism, understanding and assessment of the inherited C-suite talent is an obvious priority. If you're a new CEO, you face an immediate conundrum—even if your team has been acknowledged as requiring change, you're dependent on this inherited team, at least initially. You cannot afford to work for long with people whose work styles sharply conflict with yours, nor can you abide people whose skills are either insufficient or badly aligned with your plans. Adding to this conundrum is that the board will have a view of the senior team, but their perspective is based on less than perfect information and full of bias, since they only see the senior team in highly curated meetings. Also, they know little of how the senior team will match your personal leadership style and expectations.

As the new CEO, you need to be assessing the strength of the group throughout the due diligence and hiring process. You will need to understand the connections these executives have to board members and understand the degree of freedom you have to make changes in your own senior team.

The Reality behind Corporate Reputation/Representations. When an executive search firm or a board of directors wants to attract a potential CEO, it is to be expected that they will paint an overly flattering picture of the company—and it's rare that the story that is outlined for a potential CEO is sufficient or complete. New CEOs must challenge the reality that has been portrayed for them. Most incoming CEOs know how to conduct their own operational due diligence, assessing the market and operational success of the company, the institutional and individual talent they're inheriting, balance sheet assets and liabilities, and so on. But they need to go beyond this basic assessment and pay special attention to the following:

Financial Due Diligence. First, review of financials is obviously necessary. For some, this is where the due diligence starts and stops, and if that's the case, it's a recipe for failure. Most financials are in the public domain, but just because this information is available doesn't mean it provides a full and complete picture. Seasoned CEO candidates will go deeper than published reports of revenue growth, profitability, cash flow, debt capacity, dividend policies, and so forth. Being prepared means having examined more granular issues such as quality of earnings, supply chain economics, the match of performance trend lines with industry shifts, nature and type of debt and accompanying covenant limitations that might exist, and so forth. As one grizzled CFO veteran, who provided aid to an old friend's CEO search related, "I know that the real picture isn't in the front of the annual report. My investigation starts with all the footnotes and goes deeper from there to deliver a fuller picture of what (his friend) was going to encounter when he took the job."

Major Legal Risk Factors. All major corporations have legal exposures; there's nothing unusual about that, and this is to be expected. Yet, the frequency and nature of these legal challenges are telling signs of deeper operational problems and possibly the risk tolerance of the company. The nature of the challenges and the sources of legal issues are an important indicator of the aggressiveness of the company about its suppliers, channels, customers, employees, and so forth. You need to be especially vigilant about investigating the history of SEC and/or FTC filings. Look for filings that signal actions that are not in the norm and seek to understand what they might signal about the deeper challenges facing the company.

What Sources Can Be Used?

Look for Information in the Public Domain. You can do quite a bit on your own thanks to the huge amount of information that is readily available online, in regulatory filings, and in analyst reports. Social media sites, third-party reviews/white papers, and tracking services, such as Hoovers, also supply useful information beyond the usual array of financial and regulatory filings. Examining websites such as Glassdoor and other social employee postings sites can help you assess the mood of the employees and the down-the-line reality of the working culture of the organization. Doing this kind of homework is the necessary first step (but only the first step) in the evaluation and assessment process.

Leverage Consulting Firms. McKinsey's industry practices carefully track are were always aware of CEO/COO openings among major industry players. I am certain the other major consulting firms all do the same. We were always happy to be approached by former clients or prospective CEO candidates to aid and provide insight about target companies. It was a win-win situation. We got to be helpful to former (or potentially new) clients now vying to take bigger roles and/or internal candidates seeking to move up and lead their organizations. We in turn showcased ourselves to these new potential CEOs, and they could see that we were prepared to invest in them, hoping that we would be retained to aid the transformation-type activities to follow. We provided this assistance well aware that some of these candidates would not be selected as CEOs but that we knew they would be grateful for our help and remember it when they did become CEOs at some point in the future.

Leverage-Friendly Investment Bankers. As in the Leidos example, investment bankers can be a highly valued "one-stop shop" for all manner of financial, shareholder, and analysts' perspectives on the company you're considering. Investment bankers, much like consulting firms, have a personal stake in establishing ties with new CEOs; they know financial restructuring and new capital structures almost always follow from CEO transitions. The IBs want CEOs who are beholden to them for the service they provide during transitions.

Capitalize on Your Professional Network. At this stage in your career, you've built a diverse and extensive personal network of industry and academic contacts. Now is the time to tap it. Contact past board members, industry insiders, former colleagues from professional associations, and others who can provide you with insights and information. Professionals in your network are most likely to tell you the most unvarnished and useful insights about the challenge of any new organization, its leadership, and the board. This network can also help search for sensitive information in a very discrete way and protect your privacy at a time you might not want it known you are considering a new CEO role. Now, as a business school professor, I suppose I have a certain bias here, but it makes sense to contact your B-school alma mater for professors who can help you understand how a certain company or industry is viewed—and maybe provide relevant business cases and background readings.

I often tap people from my B-school days, former clients, and past board members for just such information—and they prove to be helpful all the time. For example, a former client was seeking to understand the real view of the relationship his target company had with their OEM suppliers. It's often hard to get information about suppliers who work principally in the business-to-business market in which business dealings are much more private than for business-to-consumer markets. Thankfully, when I was asked to provide this kind of information, I turned to a former client who was a major CFO in this sector—and I learned more from her in 30 minutes than I could have in three days of reading analyst reports and regulatory filings.

Talk to Former Executives. Reaching out to former executives with experience with the subject company can be enormously valuable (assuming no confidentiality issues exist). They will have a bias, but their internal perspective is invaluable. You want to get the "real" story, and former employees are a great source for issues that are never said publicly but that are privately well known to be big challenges.

Competitors Can Be Helpful. Again, assuming confidentiality issues can be dealt with, talking to competitors offers fresh and enlightening perspectives you can't get from the company itself. Third parties might be better suited to have these conversations, but insights from those who compete in the same space/industry as the organization you are considering can shine light on areas that you might otherwise miss.

Next Steps—Develop a Vision and the People Who Can Make It Happen

Preparation now goes beyond active listening, generation of options, considered evaluations, and the effective due diligence that I've outlined. The final area of preparedness is *a strategic and operational plan*. You must have an informed point of view, based on hypotheses, as to what actions you would propose if you were to ascend to be CEO. Boards look for candidates who haven't just the requisite intrinsic abilities and the record of accomplishment that suggest they will be great leaders. They want to know that you think in an integrated way and have a plan. This turns the selection process from a static interview process into an active and dynamic dialogue about the expectations both the board and the CEO candidate have for the business. It also builds momentum for the CEO since he or she now has begun the dialogue with the board around required action and the process for change. This informs, sets expectations, and accelerates the required change process.

View these early plans as hypotheses—very *informed* hypotheses that act to frame the approaches one might need to consider for the business. These plans will require a careful balance between knowing what you assert is needed and the need to show flexibility and willingness to adjust based on new insights. Some CEO candidates are so focused on "selling their plans," they appear arrogant and often offend the board (not to mention veteran senior team members). Some CEO candidates, when their plans are questioned, risk being overly accommodating and can appear too passive and thus not ready for the CEO role. The challenge is to find the right balance given the board and company situation.

With a balanced perspective on your plan, you are able to provide multiple stakeholders with something tangible to which they can react. Board members, your future executive team, and others can engage you in conversation about the plan, helping you develop relationships and momentum for change.

So how can this process of "arriving prepared" play out? Here are two separate stories of many that show the variety of both positive and challenging situations that can come with these critical transitions.

Jim Kilts Arrives at Gillette With a Plan

Nabisco, well known for its cookie and cracker business, hired Kilts as its president and chief executive officer in 1998. Kilts wasted little time before he began making significant changes. Shortly after assuming the CEO role he announced that the company would lay off over three thousand employees and shift considerable amounts of the savings into a focused marketing repositioning effort supported by new advertising and sales efforts. Kilts' strategies worked. He was credited with having revitalized many of Nabisco's core products and successfully positioned the company for sale. Philip Morris purchased Nabisco in 2000 for nearly $15 billion, and Kilts sought out his next CEO role.

Gillette, which had experienced several years of lackluster performance, was looking for a new CEO and was willing to go away from internal candidates for the first time in nearly 70 years. The company hired Kilts in 2001 based on his decisive management style and track record. "Jim Kilts has one of the best track records in the entire consumer products sector," said Richard R. Pivirotto, the non-executive chairman of Gillette's board. "His broad-based consumer marketing background and decisive management style make him uniquely qualified to lead The Gillette Company into an era of sustained, profitable growth" (Business Wire, January 22, 2001).

Gillette was best known for its razors and blades and men's grooming business, but it could have been better described as a holding company or a diversified packaged goods company. Its other businesses included Braun (small appliances), Duracell (batteries), and Oral-B (dental hygiene products for consumers and professionals). What did these various companies have in common? Not much. By the early 2000s, Gillette's stock was languishing. Kilts knew that with his selection the board and the company were seeking radical change.

Kilts made sure to do his "CEO-in-waiting homework" with the help of some powerful resources. Kilts reached out to, and got support from, both Bain and McKinsey consulting firms to look in depth at all the businesses that made up Gillette and to help outline a major transformative plan. His perspective, as an outsider, combined with this preparatory research yielded a strategy-shaping hypothesis: Gillette's companies should be considered a diversified portfolio that needed to be actively pruned and optimized while costs reduced substantially.

Duracell and Braun were designated for sale as they had greater value to others than to Gillette. To manage costs, Kilts immediately introduced a zero overhead growth (ZOG), policy which aimed to control costs and then invest savings in research, product development, and marketing. Kilts also wanted to boost the company's prospects for long-term health. That required a program entitled "functional excellence" (FE). As he wrote in a later book entitled *Doing What Matters*, this was "a broad-gauge initiative to achieve best-in-class capability and performance at the best possible cost." He would later add a final dimension which he called "total innovation" (TI), a program of continuous improvement, incremental innovation, and "big bang" innovation meant to come up with game-changing products.

After a successful turnaround of the various businesses yet with the prospect of limited futures for most, other than razor and blades, Kilts looked for an exit and a buyer. That buyer turned out to be Procter and Gamble, who bought Gillette for $57 billion in 2005. While employees and the city of Boston may have felt burned by the sale, it produced a great financial result for shareholders—and for Kilts.

Gary Rodkin: What He Wished He Could Have Known

Gary Rodkin was head of PepsiCo North America in 2004–2005 when the opportunity arose to become CEO of Conagra Foods. He had previously turned down a COO role at another major packaged goods company, since as he was reluctant to leave his role as head of NA and with it the opportunity to perhaps become the CEO of PepsiCo. A year later, though, he was offered the CEO job of Conagra Foods. A delegation of board members flew out to meet Gary while he was on vacation and to sell him on the role.

Gary had to balance the certainty and lost opportunity of a CEO role at a major, well-respected packaged goods company like Pepsico with the risk of moving to Omaha to take on the CEO role with a $16 billion diversified food company like Conagra Foods. As Gary was being recruited to the role he was able to defer his decision for a few weeks so that he could do his due diligence. In addition to accessing the considerable amount of information in the public domain, he spoke to a variety of former Conagra Foods management that he knew through Pepsi and industry contacts. He sought the counsel of investment bankers on the buy and sell side. He leveraged the views of management consultants and talked with competitors and customers and other industry participants. He spoke with competitors about their view of the opportunity and challenge of leading Conagra Foods. Finally, he met individually with many of the board members.

After this due diligence, he had what he described as a "full-game plan," which included transformation plans with major business portfolio adjustments, rebasing earnings, changing dividend policies, and eliminating and replacing many of the C-suite team. "These were not minor tweaks," Gary recalled. "These were fundamental and, in many cases, seismic changes to the business." With the plan in hand he gained the support of the board and accepted the CEO role with confidence that he would "arrive prepared."

In short, Gary did everything right. In most instances, this intense preparation would have helped him deal effectively with many of the complexities and uncertainties that come with the CEO position. Unfortunately, all his due diligence failed to uncover that the company's manufacturing and supply chain assets were in surprisingly poor shape and in need of massive capital upgrades/investments and that a paucity of integrated IT systems and a near total lack of integrated MIS information and decision systems made matters even worse. As a result, Gary's transition and initial tenure as CEO was beset by challenges in systems and supply chain.

"It wasn't for lack of trying because I did what I could from the outside," Gary recalled. "I don't blame the board. They didn't have 'line of sight' into the state of the manufacturing plant of the company."

"Had I known what I found out later, I would have done many things differently," Gary somewhat wistfully recalled. "The board had no real understanding of the real state of the business and the substandard level of the underlying physical plant of the company." Rodkin believed he had done his homework well, and he certainly arrived prepared, but as he cautions, "You can never know everything about a new role, but you must try and dig hard because there is always more to learn."

These two stories represent both the opportunity and challenge of leadership transitions. Those who have done this before like Kilts are "down the learning curve" and sufficiently experienced to know the core elements of due diligence requiring the greatest attention. Thus, practice makes for better outcomes here, as it does in most skilled activities.

The experience of Rodkin showcases the degree of difficulty of these transitions for new CEOs. By any measure, Rodkin did what was necessary and the appropriate due diligence. He took time and networked with others, he learned as much as he could before "getting inside the tent." Unfortunately, not only are sources of information imperfect, but many are also not as fully transparent as one would hope. Lacking the full picture, Rodkin didn't learn the whole truth of what was awaiting his arrival as a new CEO.

It Helps to Be Skeptical

As Gary Rodkin's story illustrates, there are unknowns for the best-prepared CEOs. Being as deeply and widely prepared as possible isn't a panacea, but it increases the odds that you'll deal with surprises successfully.

Perhaps his last line captures the essence of how CEOs should approach preparation and bears repeating: "You can never know everything about a new CEO role, but you must try." Gary tried harder than most, taking nearly a month to learn as much as he could about the company and the job. Despite talking to everyone from analysts to former Conagra employees, no one told him that the supply chain was seriously compromised. And even though search firms insist that they provide a clear and full picture, they often don't—sometimes because they don't know—often because it is not their job to communicate more than what they have been told by the board and the senior management team. Thus, you can never know all the unknowns, but you must do your best to uncover as many of them as possible.

One of the biggest surprises you'll face is a lack of honesty on the part of the people with which you interact. Many will tell you half-truths, others will shade the truth, and executives will position their version of events to advantage their own positions, often at the expense of full transparency. Unfortunately, barriers to truth also begin on day one of a CEO's tenure.

2

Avoid Half-Truths and Misperceptions

If you examine failed CEOs' histories, you'll nearly always find a major contributing factor: Leaders acted without sufficient or complete understanding of key information.

This doesn't seem to make sense—at first. CEOs have the position power, authority, influence, and all manner of tools to get the information they need to make informed decisions. A difficult-to-hear reality is that vast numbers of CEOs operate with partial, incomplete, biased, or heavily shaded facts and representations of the situation they seek to address. CEO position power comes with the expectation these leaders can deliver results, but most lack the complete, unbiased, fully integrated information required to make critical decisions.

A colleague who was in the Navy told me a quick story that illustrates how savvy leaders recognize that they may not be getting all the facts. A senior admiral related that when he came onto the bridge of a major aircraft carrier, he knew two things with *absolute certainty*: He was never going to get handed a cold cup of coffee, and he was never going to hear the whole truth. Useful advice for all CEOs.

The organization's natural hierarchy, human nature/ psychology, and the stresses of managerial decision-making create barriers to truth telling. In most managerial hierarchies, employees wish to please their leaders and fear that the full and complete truth, not appropriately framed and balanced, is unlikely to further their careers. Human behavior drives people to focus on the positive rather than the negative; most want to share good news, not the challenging news. All managerial decision-making requires trade-offs, and it is much easier to share options rather than address the underlying, often conflicting, positive as well as negative analyses, which are needed to ensure balanced decision-making.

Political, military, and social history is filled with examples of leaders receiving contrasting and biased perspectives from those who report to them, which often leads to failure. The situation in corporations is no different.

WHEN GOOD NEWS IS BAD ADVICE

I experienced this challenge of truth telling early on in my career. One of the most vivid examples occurred when I was serving General Motors in the 1980s. At that time Chrysler had launched a wildly successful minivan which had stolen share from General Motors and created a whole new segment in the passenger auto market. GM management knew they had to respond. GM took their commercial van and made a number of adjustments to make it into a passenger van and used it as a stop gap as they rushed to design a competitive minivan. GM designers and engineers developed what was to become known as the "dust buster" minivan, so named because of its distinctive front end, which had a massive windshield that created a dust buster–like angled/pointed front end to the vehicle.

The engineers were anxious to get consumer reactions to this new and exciting design and so took the concept car to a "car clinic" where several hundred prospective minivan owners were allowed to look at this new concept vehicle and compare it to other offerings in the market. The results were deeply disappointing. Consumer reactions were brutal. As one participant, a high school history teacher, memorably said during the focus group that followed the viewing, "Looking out at the sea of glass from the driver's seat suggests to me of how Vasco Balboa must've felt as he looked out over the Pacific Ocean." Another observed that "If they placed their sunglasses on top of the dash and went down a hill they would have to wait until they went uphill for the glasses to be returned to them." It was a disastrous outcome.

Yet, on the plane ride home there was a discussion among the engineers as to how best represent the data to senior management. What was surprising was the degree to which the data was massaged, positioned, summarized to make it sound far less of the disappointment than it was. In the subsequent debrief with the key senior executives of North America I was surprised and disappointed at the lack of candor as to the results. (When asked my summary, I was far more negative. My advice was dismissed because of my youth and lack of design expertise.) The design was adopted and was a huge disappointment in the market. (Even today a Google search under *dust buster minivan* will showcase this product.)

This challenge is not confined to the operational details. It can pertain to larger strategic issues as well. For instance, I was contacted by the general counsel of a West Coast professional service firm that was engaged in merger talks with a Midwest competitor. I was told the talks were well advanced and the deal only required that "a few details be ironed out"; they were seeking consultative counsel on how to consummate and enact the upcoming merger. The details to be finalized included the decision to locate the headquarters on the West Coast and the CEO/chairman split—the West Coast CEO would become the CEO of the combined firm, and the Midwest CEO would become chairman for a short period. Finally, the West Coast firm's name would come first on the newly combined firm name. I was assured that these details had been communicated and agreed to by the Midwest CEO and that the merger conversations were ready to accelerate.

When I spoke with the general counsel for the Midwest company, he too told me that it was "almost a done deal" and that all the communications of the details had been shared with his CEO. He then went on to add that his company's expectation was that the merged company would be located in the Midwest, their CEO would lead the new organization, and that their name would be the primary one. I wasn't shocked to discover this miscommunication. I sensed neither general counsel wanted to tell their CEO the truth. They knew that these details could precipitate explosive disagreements, sinking the deal they both had sought.

I booked a dinner reservation for the two CEOs and said to them both, "Here are three questions you both have to answer before proceeding on a deal plan:

- Who is going to be the CEO?
- Where will the company be headquartered?
- What will be the name of the firm?"

They had dinner and were shocked to discover that the deal that seemed imminent was nothing of the kind. They separately had their general counsels call me to say, "They can't agree on the basics, so no deal."

This vignette illustrates that a truth that should have been obvious—the irreconcilable conflicts created by a merged company—were hidden from CEOs. The general counsels weren't being disingenuous; they thought that a merger would be good for both organizations and wanted to make it happen. In their minds, they were being optimistic that the "details" could be worked out and that both companies would find a way to negotiate a deal that addressed these and other obvious conflicts. The CEOs, though, were operating on the assumption that their general counsels were being completely transparent about the agreement on who was going to be the

CEO, the headquarters location, and the firm name preference. Instead, the general counsels were soft-pedaling the conflicts still to be negotiated in order keep the talks moving forward.

In this instance, no harm was done because of the failed merger, but if word had leaked to the markets, clients, and media that the companies were in talks, the odds are such that they both would have been in play and become the target of other companies seeking acquisitions or mergers.

IT TAKES TWO TO TANGO: CEOs ARE PART OF THE DANCE AROUND THE TRUTH

This type of information deficiency is a well-known phenomenon within hierarchy-based organizations. Surprisingly, however, many CEOs are in denial about this reality. Many CEOs are unaware of or in denial about the significant barriers to the free flow of information between themselves and their organizations. Many new leaders, after the fact, learn what more seasoned CEOs do come to know—many interactions with their staffs rarely yield the "whole unvarnished truth." Sadly (even after interventions), the most seasoned and savvy leaders come to know that no amount of remedial action will result in their getting all the truth, all the time.

In preparation for this book, I have interviewed many CEOs on this (and other topics). Almost inevitably, this issue of truth telling grabs the attention of the leaders being interviewed. Almost all express the following sentiment: "This is an incredibly important point and something you must say to other aspiring and soon-to-be CEOs!" They then go on to add, "But of course my situation was so different: I always got the 'real story.'" In my experience, this is often not the case. CEOs are in denial even as they're recognizing the validity of this hard truth.

My fear is that you will read this and say to yourself, "Solid advice, and I hope other people listen, but here at ABC company, things are different. I understand how that could happen,

but I am a different sort of leader, and this won't happen to me."
Please beware!

Whether you're a long-tenured leader or new to the
role, you are likely to believe you won't fall victim to what
you've observed in others. It also doesn't matter whether
you're running a huge corporation, an NGO, or an academic
institution. Further, this is not just a US phenomenon driven
by the unique complexities of a domestic marketplace, but a
global one. Indeed, one consulting truism is that when you
hear from a client that incomplete and insufficient information
"has certainly been a problem with others and/or is an issue
with another, but we are, or I am, different," rest assured this
a warning sign that these underlying issues may exist.

CEOs may cause or contribute to this problem unwittingly.
Leaders who aren't open to others or willing to hear contrarian
views cause people to adjust their views or edit their remarks.
By not actively encouraging and welcoming the telling of bad
news, you compound and perpetuate an already prevalent
problem. Without affirming and reinforcing that you want
"transparency and debate," members of your executive team
are likely to avoid offering complete or timely information, or
they will hedge the information they share to put the news in
its most positive light. Power renders information incomplete
or inaccurate when that power is used punitively rather than
used with purpose and care.

EXAMPLES OF DAMAGING HALF-TRUTHS
AND WITHHELD INFORMATION

Shortly after Jim Kilts took over as CEO of Gillette, he began
meeting with community leaders and attending community
forums, speaking about his vision for Gillette and celebrating
the company's long history with Boston. He publicly spoke
about the financial contributions Gillette had made to Boston.
A few months after assuming this role, Jim joined a dinner of
other local CEOs and community and political leaders I host

at my home. During the dinner, Jim reiterated his beliefs about Gillette and Boston. One of the CEOs in the room, taking advantage of the privacy of the dinner, confronted Jim and said, "You have to got to stop saying that; it is simply not true (and went on to say why Gillette's history wasn't as portrayed), and you're losing credibility by repeating it so frequently." Others around the table concurred, and Jim was chastened and surprised. A few days later Jim called to thank me not only for the dinner but also for the candor in the room; it provided the insight and impetus for him to ask his team tough questions about Gillette's role in the city and get a more complete and nuanced view of how their community efforts and standing were viewed. He didn't need to tell me that his staff hadn't been forthcoming prior to that dinner—it was clear to all of us at the dinner, as it had happened in some manner to everyone there.

Organizational structure, too, can hide pieces of the picture. Keurig/Green Mountain Coffee enjoyed tremendous success with the introduction of the Keurig coffee brewing system and single pod coffee offering. They revolutionized both commercial and private home approaches to preparing and consuming coffee. When the new CEO, Brain Kelly, came to the company from Coke, he catalyzed new growth through expanded coffee offerings via many innovative partnerships. He also prepared the company for the next tranche of growth by planning to introduce a cold beverage soda brewing system. Brian was focused on creating partnerships critical to near-term growth and building a new management team and negotiating with Coke, who wanted a major equity stake in the company. He was reliant on his staff to keep him abreast of the activity to deliver on the promise of a holiday launch of the new cold soda machine. As a result, Brian wasn't made fully aware of the dysfunctionality of the effort to bring the new product forward. Because of Keurig's matrixed structure, the project lead didn't have the power to override the competing interests of the siloed groups, such as engineering, manufacturing, and design. Procurement challenges abounded, and the training of an expanded sales force was having major challenges. In the routine launch reviews the situation was portrayed as challenged and that roadblocks were evident but that the program effort was "addressing them."

Brian thought he was getting the full picture, but instead it was fragmented and segregated and heavily shaded to the positive. So Brian was aware the introduction faced challenges, but he wasn't aware of how deep those challenges ran. The product was launched with major fanfare at critical home shows in advance of the holiday period, and analysts had high expectations. The product arrived in the market late, over budget, and had major design flaws, producing poor consumer reviews. It was to be one of the most disappointing launches of a new small appliance in recent years. Even now after the sale of Keurig to a PE Firm, I am sure Brian is asking, "Why weren't my staff more forthcoming? Why didn't I push harder to know more sooner?"

Lest we think these illustrations are outliers, consider some recent corporate disasters and how and why management responded as it did—were truths really being told? Do we think VW engineers were fully forthcoming about their diesel testing approach? Do we think Wells Fargo retail bank management was open with senior management about the impact of their incentives to cross-sell products and their use of phantom accounts? Were "down the line" pharmaceutical distributors of opioids transparent to their management teams about their outsized shipment to specific regions of the country where disproportionally larger opioid addiction rates existed? Was the GE board of directors fully informed as to the state of the power generation business that eventually imploded and helped to force a dramatic turnaround of this iconic American company? Did the Boeing Max 737 team fully disclose their approach to safety testing?

At Harvard Business School we teach specific cases that highlight this management challenge. The Theranos case illustrates the lack of communication, transparency, and truth sharing between the charismatic and deeply flawed CEO

Elizabeth Holmes and her high-profile board of advisors. Lost in this story of deceit is that major channel participants, such as Walgreens, were largely duped into participating (by their own competitive desires) in what was essentially a fraud. Do we really believe that the entire truth was being shared among all elements of the Walgreens store operations as to true progress/efficiency of the Theranos joint venture?

You can overcome the barriers to gathering relevant information if you encourage people to funnel all types of news your way and take ongoing actions that plug you into what's happening in the organization.

Unfortunately, this approach to leadership is not standard operating procedure and takes a great deal of humility and openness that many CEOs might see as weakness. Instead, business leaders too often find themselves one, two, and sometimes several very critical steps removed from the actual inner workings of their own companies. CEOs want to believe they are getting adequate information, and it requires real discipline to assume that they are not getting the uncomfortable news and push to receive it. It is human nature to want to "stay with the positive" rather than "confront the negative."

I experienced the power of truth telling early in my career as a young manager at McKinsey. Our firm had been retained by Bristol Meyers at a time when they had a large consumer products business, including Clairol Products and a large over-the-counter (OTC) division selling Bayer Aspirin and Ban personal care products. The general manager of the OTC business (then called the Products Division) retained McKinsey to solve a vexing business riddle: why the retail sales of their OTC products to consumers were steady, yet at the same time their sales into the "trade" (i.e., the wholesalers and intermediaries and retailers that buy product from Bristol Myers and "break bulk" and supply retail outlets) were softening at a worrisome rate. The Bristol Myers management team suspected that the trade *must have been liquidating* inventories and changing their inventory polices and stocking less OTC products. The OTC business unit head hired us to find out why the trade was liquidating inventories. The unit head was relying on his management team's input that the trade's buying behavior was the underlying cause of declining performance.

At the very outset of our work we asked, "How long had the trade been taking this action?" They told us 3–5 months. How could this be? we thought. It would be highly unusual for the trade to have had that amount of inventories in the system to deplete.

We used brand management modeling tools to understand the sales and trade dynamics of the past few years. We also visited major buyers and checked warehouses to examine the inventories of Bristol Meyers products. We quickly came to a disturbing conclusion: Rather than depleting inventories, the trade was *building* inventories and was soon going to stop buying any more products at all.

Their internal brand teams were using flawed models and forecasts that relied on revenue rather than unit sales, as this was the means by which they were being incentivized. The myopic revenue focus obscured issues of inflation, trade mix, and trade promotions—all of which affected the actual numbers of packages, bottles, and pills that were being sold into the trade.

The slight disquiet felt by executives after a few weeks of low sales to the trade *should have* turned to alarm. The executives should *not* have required a third party to tell them what they likely sensed. They should have said, "Sales to the trade are down precipitously; we have no time to lose to figure out this problem in detail." But down the line executives at Bristol Myers didn't share their concerns and continued to rely on the more positive revenue share focus in their communication with the senior management team.

Our formal presentation of findings proved beyond any analytical doubt that the situation was dire. The product division *had too much inventory*, and we predicted an imminent sales drop. Upon hearing this, the general manager of the OTC division looked slightly stunned and eventually turned to my senior colleague and asked, "In your experience what happened to others that faced this situation?" My colleague did not hesitate: "Well," he said, "when the *new* management team is hired, they usually do the following things to correct such strategic errors . . . ."

It was a brutal message, but it was the truth. Indeed, sales did plummet over the next few quarters, the general manager and much of his team were released, and eventually, several years later, the entire portfolio of Bristol Myers OTC products was sold. Why didn't the Bristol sales team and brand team speak up? Why was the general manager left so exposed? Many were to blame—the sales and marketing people justified their lack of complete candor by saying they addressed the questions asked by their senior management team. They figured that if the general manager wanted to know more of the details of the business situation, he would ask. They both failed one another.

KNOW YOUR SHAKESPEARE, DON'T BE LIKE LEAR

The truth may hurt, but it hurts even more when you make decisions based on misleading versions of the truth. Therefore, never discourage people from bringing you bad news. The CEOs I have worked with who foster transparency and open debate of alternative views actively encourage the "bad news." Bad news can and should be welcomed, as it is often the most valuable feedback about how to correct strategy. If problems are discovered early on, and taken seriously, recovery is almost always possible, while obfuscation and delay almost certainly cause failure.

Our reflex to please and pamper leaders rather than risk upsetting them with bad news is deeply ingrained, and it's encouraged (consciously or not) by leaders. Shakespeare dramatized these behaviors in *King Lear*. Lear is reluctant to yield his throne and distribute his wealth among his three daughters. To determine how to make this allocation, the king asks his daughters directly who loves him the most. Lear, like many CEOs, enjoys hearing good news from everybody. And the testimony from his first two daughters, Goneril and Regan, is what Lear wants to hear: They love him more than anyone and with all their hearts.

But Lear's youngest daughter (i.e., the most rebellious of the "management team"), Cordelia, demurs. When pressed about why she won't tell him what he wants to hear, Cordelia gives Lear a realistic forecast: When she is married, she will be as devoted to her husband as she is to her father. She's careful to say this is not a sign of disrespect or lack of thankfulness to her father but just a truthful assessment of changes that will take place soon. Lear responds bitterly, telling his daughter that truth is all well and good, but it will cost her her inheritance.

Like Lear, CEOs of all types and all size companies and operations must face issues of poor communication between leaders and followers—poor communication that may result in half-truths, obfuscations, and shading of the truths. In Shakespeare's play, two of the king's three daughters felt compelled to shade the truth and tell him what they thought he hoped to hear.

As an advisor to CEOs facing difficult decisions, I have experienced this problem firsthand. Unfortunately many clients/leaders are reluctant to hear the unwelcome truths that a third-party objective analysis uncovers. Because of this unwillingness, I have had clients suffer huge failures introducing major new products; a decline of brand equity and the loss of hundreds of millions of dollars; bitter fights and feuds among C-level executives that were unknown to the CEO; and, of course, the firing and sometimes the humiliation of CEOs themselves.

A firm's organizational structure can reinforce the reflex to hide bad news. Large organizations have historically depended on hierarchical structures of relationships—often represented by detailed organizational charts—to delineate roles and responsibilities, especially, who is accountable to whom. While these organizational structures promote efficiency and role clarity, they usually don't encourage the sharing of information and transparency. In fact, if the flow of information within a company principally follows the paths delineated by "org charts" (which is the case in many companies), information sharing "between the lines" of those charts can be (bureaucratically speaking) very challenging. When our inclination to hide bad news is reinforced by organizational design, the truth can easily be missed, misunderstood, or conveniently tucked away in a silo or corner of an organization's culture.

Another challenge to transparency of information: the difficulty of gaining an integrated view of the organization. Staffs can, and strive to, report accurately on their team, department, business unit or function, but many will be hesitant to share a more integrated view of issues that involve multiple perspectives. Relying on information gathered only from "silos" fails to provide a full accounting of any specific situation or key decision. I often find myself repeating to clients: "The vertical flow of information is not your problem." Staffs often share their views about their directly assigned functions and business units. The problem is more often "the horizontal," where fewer executives have the information, intuition, or willingness to take the risk of providing integrative perspectives that describe the challenge not just for a unit/function but for the corporation as a whole.

CEOs must acknowledge that they can't know everything and that they must rely on their chief lieutenants for information, counsel, and advice. They can and need to encourage contrarian or alternative views, and by accepting these views without rancor or admonitions they can foster an atmosphere that encourages candor and a collective culture where everybody speaks up. The simplest way for a CEO to do that is to listen more and talk less. Unfortunately, some top leaders talk more and listen less, a fatal flaw in a managerial era where more information than ever is required before increasingly complex decisions need to be made.

CEOs can certainly model transparency and behaviors to encourage their staffs to share integrated perspectives and take risks to communicate good and bad news equally. However, a number of other factors act as roadblocks to this culture of transparency and risk taking.

Corporations by necessity strive to represent themselves in the most positive possible light to emphasize good news and minimize negative trends, not choosing to overly focus on the obstacles to achieving strategic and operational objectives. There are many stakeholders (analysts, shareholders, activists, board members, and other executives) who expect—and sometimes seem to demand—a constant stream of news that they hope and assume will be focused on positive developments. Investor pressure for continuous improvement is intense. Annual public updates, shareholder meetings, SEC filings, analyst reports, investor conferences all are positioned to put a company's numbers (and underlying operations) in the best light possible. This need to "position" the information for external audiences can also discourage transparency and deep debate among an executive management team when sharing internal information and results. It's natural for management to assume that they want to align their internal messaging with their external messaging, taking comfort they are doing what the corporation needs and the CEO requires by being careful in the way they balance the positive and the negative.

The good news is that embracing the truth can pay really big dividends for your company and its employees, and it's a "tactic" we'll explore later. For now, though, be aware that the flow of candid information to a CEO tends to be more the exception than always the rule. If we are to move confidently toward creating a company and a culture that encourages truth telling, we need to be aware of some common barriers that impede honest communication.

Roadblock #1: Believing Too Much in Your Past Success

It's not only lonely at the top, but it's also isolating. When you first become CEO or the leader of a major organization, you lose touch with your formerly reliable networks of information cultivated as a lower-level executive. Even after being CEO for months or years, it is easy to remain isolated. The position itself acts as a deterrent to honest feedback. Consequently, CEOs often rely on "what brought them to the dance"—the strategies, models, and ideas that brought them success earlier in their careers.

We teach a case at HBS that illustrates this problem. Ron Johnson was considered by many to be a marketing genius who had a huge positive impact as the chief marketer at Apple and Target, before joining J. C. Penny as the CEO.

Johnson is best known for his Apple retail store design concept featuring popular customer service innovations such as the in-store "genius bar." At Target, Johnson was the merchandiser who came up with a lot of the Target "high design" products that made the retail chain so successful, including the Graves product line. But the trajectory of his business accomplishments took a dramatically negative turn when he became CEO of J. C. Penney, where he stayed on for just 17 months (November 2011 to April 2013).

Johnson's "turnaround" strategy for J. C. Penney ran counter to traditional retail principles; he sought to avoid coupons, lowered prices but not so low that they were the lowest prices (thus failing to compete on cost), and shifted away from promotion and other traditional sales techniques. Even more challenging was the idea of establishing boutique stores within a store, which seemed out of step with the traditional J. C. Penney shopper. More disastrous was rolling out his strategy quickly without any testing—even in advance of completing new store designs! Most observers agree that these were major mistakes.

When Johnson visited our MBA classroom, he was candid in admitting that there were many aspects to the CEO position that he had not appreciated before, such as living under the microscopic gaze of many stakeholders and the lack of flexibility of the organization he inherited. When he was asked to explain the key reason why he failed, he used the phrase, "situational arrogance."

I interpreted that term to mean that he applied the retail lessons he learned at Apple to the very different retail realities of J. C. Penney. Doing this was ill advised because the two companies live in totally different retail universes. The average sale at J. C. Penney is $63. It's a middle market business where a lot of the interaction with consumers happens on the retail sales floor. The average sale at Apple is over $600 with a brand that carries the high tech factor and has established loyalty among consumers long before they enter an Apple retail outlet.

Johnson admitted he was overconfident/possibly arrogant because of his previous situation, where he had been enormously successful. Because of the natural isolation of CEOs deprived of traditional peer networks—networks that might level with CEOs and provide reality checks—Johnson operated with the past as his primary guide.

What is often overlooked in this story is that when Johnson came to J. C. Penny he did so with several "chief lieutenants" who had previously worked with him at either Target or Apple, people he had chosen to work with him in this new endeavor. He also chose to work with former J. C. Penny executives who were very familiar with the traditional customers and relationships with suppliers that had once been central to J. C. Penny success. The question needs to be asked: Why didn't these key executives push back on Johnson's strategy that seemed so likely to fail? Why did they hesitate when they were chosen lieutenants from his former companies or retained executives from J. C. Penny? At least one of them must have thought that some of his hasty moves were likely to fail. Why didn't they counteract Johnson's "situational arrogance"?

Their new situation at J. C. Penney placed them in a weaker position in relation to Johnson than they had occupied at Apple and Target. They may have feared that if they displayed candor at J. C. Penney they wouldn't be seen as team players or part of the new, conquering leadership team that "knew what was right." If they were retained executives from J. C. Penny, they may have feared they didn't have the "standing" to question the CEO who was so determined to strike out in a new direction. As Johnson came under intense pressure from the board and activists, who knew if he might lash out at a truth teller. Whether these fears were real or imagined, the effect was the same—they must have muted their assessments or provided overly positive feedback.

As Johnson left the HBS classroom, I wanted my students to remember another important lesson from this case so they might avoid Johnson's mistakes in their own careers as leaders. "All of you, let me remind you of one thing: It's a hell of a lot harder to be a CEO than to be the head of marketing." And in saying those words, the lesson rang home to me more clearly than ever. Ron Johnson was a great executive. He was a great marketer. But despite all that success in business, perhaps even because of all that success, he made mistakes caused by the inherent, isolating nature of the CEO job. He didn't have all the information he needed to make the right decisions—not because he didn't want all the information but because the job itself made it difficult to obtain it.

Roadblock #2: Unwilling to Acknowledge Frightening Realities

Another older story from GM helps illustrate this point. Its lesson is probably even more relevant today given how scary the current environment is—and how easy it is to ignore or deny what scares us. In the 1980s, General Motors was an industrial powerhouse. It sold over 40 percent of all automobiles and light trucks in the US, and it was the largest and most prominent manufacturing company in the US economy. Toward the end of the decade, CEO Roger Smith retired, and the new management team of Robert Stemple and Lloyd Reuss ascended to the top two jobs at GM by 1990. Stemple was the new CEO, and Reuss was in charge of all domestic operations.

At this time, the threat from Japanese imports was becoming very real, and the market dominance GM had enjoyed for decades was weakening. McKinsey (and I was a lead on the team) was retained by GM to examine a wide variety of emerging challenges in the US sales and marketing arenas.

Time and time again our analyses and review of operations highlighted the shortsightedness of the senior management team's almost singular obsession with market share. Market share was increasingly being obtained by low-cost financing, rebates, dealer incentives, and fleet sales, all of which meant that the quality of GM's earnings was declining. In short, these policies were hollowing out the business. While share of market might remain stable, the underlying margins per vehicle were rapidly weakening, and the threat to earnings was becoming deeply worrisome.

This situation was discussed extensively with, and to a large degree understood by, the general managers of the various "Nameplate Divisions" (i.e., Chevrolet, Pontiac, Oldsmobile, Cadillac, Buick, and GMC), all of whom reported directly to Reuss. Time and time again we urged the Nameplate executives to share the deteriorating position of the US marketing efforts with other GM senior corporate executives and with Reuss. We found it challenging to get these individuals to lay out the full story of the worsening competitive situation. Some were unconvinced that the market share focus was to blame, others wanted to stay in the "good graces" of the new management team, and there were those who thought the rest of the general managers were to blame and that their particular division wasn't the culprit, and their line of cars or light trucks was successful. No matter what the McKinsey team argued, the full truth was never really told or at least understood by all of GM's management. It was easier to rationalize their position or deny problems than articulate a truly worsening situation.

Finally, having failed in my efforts to get these key line leaders to take the message forward, I met with Reuss on this topic. I explained the need for a dramatic shift away from a singular focus on volume to one balanced by margin concerns. We spoke of the "hollowing out" of the earnings picture and that a focus on market share obtained by rebates and low-interest loans was creating a cycle of decline. In particular, we spoke about the increasing practice of selling new vehicles to rental fleets that were then bought back at the end of short three- to six-month leases only to be resold into the secondary used car market (through auctions), thus causing further downward pressure on prices. I summed up the problem bluntly for him: "You are 'renting your market share,' and you will ultimately lose."

Reuss, like many GM executives at the time, responded with an all-too-GM familiar refrain of "I hear you," but he really didn't. He understood what I was saying, but he was unable to fully grasp the frightening reality that he faced, perhaps because I was a lone voice (and a young one and an outsider who wasn't a "true car guy"), and his people weren't communicating the same message. I recall Reuss saying repeatedly that if he could only get market share back to 40 percent, then all would be fine. I recall warning him that his position as head of US operations was at risk. Unfortunately, his job was indeed at risk, and Reuss was released in 1992.

Some corporations have managed to integrate truth telling into their culture—they identify challenging realities immediately without fear of repercussions. The Toyota production system is often held up as an example of how truth telling leads to sharp increases in quality and efficiency. In this system, factory workers are encouraged, empowered, and rewarded to call out concerns about defects they see in the assembly line. They are empowered to the point that when a significant problem is identified, they can question whether production should continue. But even Toyota has failed in recent years in maintaining transparency—this time with outside stakeholders during their US 2009 scandal concerning defective anti-lock brakes in some of their cars. Nevertheless, people return to learn from Toyota's production system so often because it's the exception that proves the rule—and the rule is, more often than not, that many company leaders would rather not hear hard truths.

Roadblock #3: The Lack of an Integrated View

I consulted for a packaged goods company that had come up with a new product with breakthrough potential. The company had invested considerable time and money in R&D, and everyone was optimistic that this could be a game-changer. Natalie, the CEO of this company, saw that this drug could bring in huge amounts of revenue for her new company, and she made it clear that her performance expectations for her staff's work on the product launch were sky-high.

My consulting focus was on the education and training of the rapidly expanding management team launch. It didn't take long to see that things weren't going as well as the company had planned and management had hoped. The new product was scheduled to go to market in December. I was supposed to work with the CEO and the head of HR to help different parts of the company collaborate more easily and become more market oriented. I wasn't retained to help specifically on the new product launch, but every training meeting ended with a deep discussion of the new product effort and the serious concerns executives had about the upcoming launch—the intensely competitive segment they hoped to address with the new product and the possibility of legal issues involving the product (a significant number of lawsuits had been filed against some key suppliers).

This was a highly siloed company, rigidly divided into business functions. Their sales force was separate from the R&D people, who were separate from the production people, who were separate from the supply chain people. They did have a project manager, who was nominally in charge of coordinating these functions, but she was overwhelmed by the day-to-day process demands of the launch and had more influence than authority. Because of this, no one in the organization ever told Natalie the hard facts—that the various functions in the organization weren't collaborating effectively and that they weren't prepared for the upcoming product launch.

From my consultant's perspective, I wanted to sound the alarm so that Natalie would hear it. Unfortunately, barriers exist that not only prevent CEOs from hearing the alarm internally but from external sources as well. I had to get the permission from the head of HR (my client) to talk to Natalie (which is another example of how companies shield CEOs from the truth). Nonetheless, I went around the head of HR, reaching out to Natalie directly (who was and remains a friend), urging her to meet me so we could discuss the problems that employees from various functions had raised with me. The head of HR never supported the outreach and was likely angry for my end run around her. The situation was such that Natalie was past the "fail-safe line," and she was committed to the plans and approach, and therefore, the time for mid-course correction had passed. The launch was a failure.

When CEOs require an integrated view of their companies, but their individual team members only see vertically into their respective business domains, they suffer from partial vision. To make the right decisions, management teams have to have good knowledge of what's going on outside of their own area of direct exposure. And to obtain that knowledge, they need to know it's okay to ask probing questions of other executives representing other parts of the corporation, and those being questioned must believe that they won't be punished for delivering bad news, revealing they made mistakes, or admitting that their part of the business underperformed in some way.

HOW TO MOVE FROM PARTIAL TO WHOLE TRUTHS

Once you understand that truth is often hidden behind ingrained habits and attitudes within a company, it may seem very daunting to reverse this culture. But it can be done. Here are five ways you can get the ball rolling. And once you start, you'll probably discover other ways to encourage truth telling vertically and horizontally in your business.

1. **Cultivate a personal style that encourages openness and frankness.** CEOs are often beset by either pride or pressure (or both) to appear infallible. This is an impossible task for any human being, and the sooner you discard this notion, the better. Realize that personal strength (meaning knowledge, competence, and encouraging trust in your organization) comes from projecting an openness to others that encourages them to address you frankly—with the good news, bad news, and the in-between. Pull people toward you by modelling this behavior *and* finding ways to reward people who bring you news of negative developments. This will demonstrate that you can be adaptable to new situations; you'll encourage others to share more information with you, which will make you a much better-informed decision-maker.

2. **Design processes to circumvent the hierarchy.** Know that a traditional organization will stop the flow of information or "smooth the edges" of recommendations so they are less crisp and clear it as it moves upward. People will share information in a way that puts themselves and their work in the best light. Instead of fighting this, open new channels of information by asking for a second or third opinion on a task or topic. To do this, ask people from different parts of the corporation (e.g., an executive team, a functional group, and a business unit) to report on the same issue. They'll all come back to you with an analysis of the subject viewed from a slightly different lens. With multiple perspectives, you can gain a clearer view of issues and situations (and avoid the problems connected with the blind spots that come with any single view of your company's performance).

3. **Use incentives to encourage openness.** One of the main barriers to truth telling in a corporation is competition for resources. With an incentive structure that encourages collaboration and not competition, there are far fewer incentives to hide underperformance or to not be transparent about challenges in any one unit. CEOs can use competition structures and the way that staff are rewarded and prompted to minimize intramural competition. So instead of being the portfolio manager with each of the business units responsible for its own P&L driving for individualized outcomes, the whole business becomes more of the focus of the management teams, and this eliminates the desire to battle for resources and succeed at the expense of another group. Executives within business units become more open with each other because they are now being rewarded from the same pool of resources.

4. **Find a way to step back and see the bigger picture.** Not to mix metaphors, but when you're too close to the bark of the tree, you can't see how tall it is. Gaining an outside perspective is crucial. Most CEOs become so enmeshed in the details of planning and strategy that they lose perspective. One tactic for stepping back and seeing the big picture is bringing in a consultant. Obviously, as a consultant, I'm not completely objective about this issue, but this isn't the only way you can gain perspective. An additional tactic may involve removing yourself (and your team) physically from the office, going off site in order to contemplate a potential major move free of the daily office routine. A third tactic may be a role-playing exercise—assign a "red team" to be the competition, and articulate how they see you. Clay Christensen, a former revered professor at HBS, believes that you must creatively destroy portions of a company in order to make it whole. A team might discuss what this creative destruction would look like and its implications. In some instances, CEOs reach out

to boards and request that they conduct independent assessment of their companies.

5. **Reward the messengers of both good and bad news.** Successful CEOs and leaders are those who not only welcome bad news but also expect it, and when they do not get it they ask, "What am I not being told?" While an observer might quickly assume that this demand to hear "bad news" is accompanied by a negative outlook and difficult personality, great leaders and accomplished CEOs can turn this line of questioning into a positive.

Great CEOs intuitively understand that executives are fallible and prone to seek favor by shading truths. They respond by being disarming, welcoming input, and asking for help. Also seasoned CEOs learn to:

A. **Acknowledge that they don't know and want to know.** If you directly or indirectly use your position of authority to emphasize to those reporting to you that you are smart and "know better," you will shut down dialogue. Instead, acknowledge the weakness and gaps in your knowledge, and see this acknowledgment as a sign of strength of character and *not* a weakness in your authority.

B. **Ask everyone without regard to hierarchy.** Accomplished leaders ask for input (including opinions) from every one of their direct reports all the time. They also ask for feedback from the executive assistants they encounter as they visit various offices. I have seen leaders engage drivers who picked them up from the airport and junior staff who would accompany CEOs as they travel from building to building. Good leaders will call former customers and suppliers to get views from the retail and supply chain front lines.

Another CEO never went into the field without seeing dealers and other front line staff.

C. **Say thank you for what they've learned.** Express gratitude for the information and knowledge received. Never ever "kill the messengers" because the word always spreads, and the flow of information from future messengers will stop quickly. Find a way to offer a positive response, even when what was heard was unexpected or negative. The value of saying, "It is really important you told me; thank you for sharing with me"; the value of asking, "What else should I know?" cannot be underestimated.

TOLERATE FAILURE, HEAR THE FULL TRUTH

In the end, truth telling within a company depends on developing some tolerance for failure. A culture that welcomes reports of failure can generate crucial information as a means to improve quality and productivity. That culture is possible to create, but it emerges after a long and deliberate effort, not wishful thinking. Few companies are willing to accept five or six CEO failures before they get to the wins. In the short term, this tolerance of failure may seem unacceptable, but it's crucial for long-term success. If you develop a culture that accepts the existence and reporting of failure, you can create a workplace where full disclosure and complete information are welcomed and used to the company's advantage.

3

Adopt a Constituent Consciousness

Most new CEOs are well aware that multiple and various stakeholders will make demands on their time, but many aren't prepared for the reality of the overwhelming volume and intensity of these demands. They often anticipate that they can manage these demands much as they did in their previous senior-level positions, or they feel confident that they can apply lessons learned from observing their CEO or other executives and feel this transition will be easily handled.

In fact, most new CEOs are shocked by the sheer volume of these demands. Customers, channel participants, buy-side and sell-side analysts, regulators, employee groups, suppliers, union organizations, alumni and retirees, vast numbers of politically connected groups, potential activists, and community leaders all clamor for CEOs' time and attention. With the advent of hour-by-hour news cycles and acceptance and use of Twitter, Instagram, and other social media, CEOs have far less control of issues that once could be more easily anticipated and managed. Instead, they are expected to react almost instantly to events that interrupt daily routines, often with no warning.

CEOs quickly discover that attempting to satisfy the conflicting demands of all these groups leads to a continual sense of feeling overwhelmed by the sheer press of activity and the effect on one's calendar. Indeed, new CEOs find that in the early stage of their transitions their calendars can be so full that they lack the time to address the operational and strategic questions that were their priorities when they became CEOs.

Also, as a previous strategic business unit (SBU) leader or another C-suite level position-, they could often leverage their direct reports to handle many of the constituencies in their particular arena. Alternatively, they could "refer" these constituents to the senior corporate leaders and more importantly, their CEO. In their previous roles, they certainly had observed some of these pressures but rarely with a full view; they were not able to fully observe the sheer breadth or the intensity of what a CEO faces. As a result, executives may have little experience with how to set priorities and the process trade-offs necessary to manage these demands. New CEOs quickly learn the reality that for many, if not most, major constituencies, the constituent in question is not satisfied unless they deal with the top person directly.

New CEOs must acknowledge, as they ascend to this top job, that they lack full visibility into all the constituencies they need to manage. They must also recognize the need to weather the initial onslaught of new demands, develop a process for setting priorities, make informed trade-offs, learn not to respond to every demand, and set limits and create contingencies—if they are to find the time to make the key operational and strategic decisions required as a newly named CEO.

CRAZY CALENDARS, MYOPIA, AND INTENSE DEMANDS

Imagine sitting in your office ready to start the day by digging into a crucial strategic issue, and your chief of staff enters and says, "You have 20 meetings booked for today and several critical messages to return." So much for addressing strategy.

Dominic Casserley, a former senior partner of McKinsey, became CEO of Willis, a large multi-billion-dollar insurance brokerage company, and shortly after he started his job there, his chief of staff gave him the "20-meetings" news. He was flabbergasted to discover just how out of control his calendar would be if not managed. More significantly, Dominic was chagrined at how difficult it was to set priorities across a vast array of constituencies, each requesting his direct and immediate attention. On top of all this, Dominic had not anticipated the intense regulatory, auditing, and shareholder demands that emerged during his first few months on the job.

Fortunately, Dominic embraced the approach of many more seasoned CEOs: triage and delegate. He quickly realized not every interaction with a constituent group is as timely as with another. Some who spoke the loudest were not always the ones with the most critical concerns. Much like an ER doctor, CEOs have to triage and set priorities with their calendar. As for leverage, their general counsel and the CFO can often work wonders through filtering and triage, especially at the beginning of CEOs' tenures. These individuals often possess the experience and expertise to help new leaders set priorities and can take on responsibilities to address varied constituencies. They possess credibility through the force of their legal and financial roles and are seen as individuals with ready access to the CEO. Even Dominic, who was a deeply experienced client counselor, a major firm leader, and head of a major geographical region—far more capable than most at dealing with external demands—found himself overwhelmed in the early days at Willis. "I thought my consulting career and experiences in other leadership roles would have had me prepared for the initial onslaught of demands. I was shocked at the sheer number of people who insisted on seeing me—my calendar was not my own for many weeks," recalled Dominic.

This risk doesn't go away just because you learn, as Dominic did, to deal with the level of complexity. The demands of constituency management can reassert themselves in the normal course of running the business. For example, consider the challenge faced by Jeff Clarke, the newly installed CEO of Kodak.

Clarke took over Kodak when it was in free fall and in crisis. Vast numbers of constituencies were anxiously lined up to lobby and suggest what Jeff should do with this iconic business. Kodak was emerging from bankruptcy and becoming an object lesson in what happens when a corporation fails to adapt. Headquartered in Rochester, New York, Kodak had been the economic and intellectual center of the upstate New York/ Rochester community, and many people in the area owed their livelihood to the once proud and innovative Kodak Corporation. Not surprisingly, the community was deeply worried about the future of the company and the significant loss of jobs and deleterious impact on the whole region if the company were to fall even further. Retirees were rightfully concerned about the loss of their pensions, and employees feared for their jobs. Regional academic institutions worried about a loss of students no longer attracted by Kodak's famous research facilities, and retailers worried about loss of income. Activists and analysts were declaring that the company should be broken apart and sold off in pieces to at least deliver some value as the company lost its market-dominant position in a digital world.

If this was not sufficiently daunting, consider that in the very first week of his becoming CEO, the board asked that Jeff provide a point of view about the advisability of shutting down a major part of Kodak—its iconic feature film business. His response was the subject of heated speculation; his point of view would not only have financial implications but would also presage the company's future strategy and its very ability to survive.

Multiple constituencies were literally hanging on his every word. They quickly came to analyze how Jeff spent his time, who Jeff spoke with, what plants he visited, who he brought into the management team, and even personal issues such as whether he would relocate his family from their

West Coast home to Rochester as signals of his commitment to the business. Such can be the intensity of constituency demands.

One need not be a CEO of a large corporate entity to face this dilemma. Consider Max Hodges, who came to Boston as the executive director of Boston Ballet. Before having ascended to this leadership role, Max had led a smaller arts organization in NYC and so had some familiarity with the nature and stress of leading a not-for-profit organization. Yet, when she arrived, she was greeted by all manner of interested parties immediately requiring her attention. Her staff wanted to know what her priorities were while the marketing staff said she had but a few days to set out how she wanted the pricing strategy to be handled for the upcoming season. The development staff wanted to have dates when she could meet with prospective donors; members of her large board of trustees were anxious for updates on what she was finding in her first few days and what her plans were for the business side of the ballet. In addition, Max's relationship with the creative side of the ballet and its artistic director had to be built, and many community leaders and local university directors (where members of the ballet company went to university) wanted to welcome and meet her. Finally, parents were calling to inquire about placements for their children in the pre-professional training program.

If this wasn't challenging enough, after a few months as executive director, Max learned that the landlord holding the lease for the largest and most profitable of three neighborhood ballet schools was cutting their lease to allow development of the building. She faced the prospect of losing a major revenue stream and having nowhere to teach over 3000 young students. Max said at the time, "I was the executive director of an arts organization in NYC and had been a management consultant for many years, but I was shocked at the sheer variety of demands on my time when I first arrived. I had to be very careful not to lose control of the critical agenda."

Jeff, Max, and Dominic are the rule, not the exception. CEOs may underestimate the demands of multiple constituencies on their time and overestimate their capacity to deal effectively with them. They may be unprepared for how the job prevents them from controlling their time as they had in the past. They may be shocked by the intense pressures these groups exert. Most will learn, as these three CEOs did, to triage, segment, and delegate and put in place processes required to meet the needs of an onslaught of constituencies. What they might not recognize, though, is the toll it will take on them individually.

I am familiar with Isabella, a CEO who chose, for important family reasons, to live far from corporate headquarters, requiring a significant daily commute. This wasn't a high-tech, low-touch environment where distance and off-site management were possible. Isabella had to be on site and her presence was central to the business. On top of that, she was a workout fanatic, devoting time every day to intense exercise. Given the organization's functional nature and Isabella's large number of direct reports, she was in constant meetings acting as an integrating force among the functional silos of the operations. Isabella also felt that her presence was critically important with key customers and carved out time to meet with many community groups and financial analysts, believing that the CEO alone could best represent the needs of the company.

While this commitment might be considered by some as admirable and appropriate, it soon took a personal toll on Isabella. Her senior staff began to notice she was unable to focus in key meetings and would catch her falling asleep in late afternoon meetings when listening to presentations. She became far more direct to the point of mean-spiritedness at times, when dealing with employee groups. Customers grumbled that Isabella lacked personality, could be overly directive, and got angry too easily. Board members intervened, offering Isabella organizational and operational assistance and even suggesting personal adjustments; they told Isabella that they would help in all these areas. Initially, Isabella may have felt accepting this help would be a sign of personal weakness. She thanked the board for its concern, promised to change her behavior, and largely continued on. To make a bad situation even worse, she was a poor delegator. Burnout and/or failure seemed inevitable.

Reading these examples, most readers will immediately recognize that delegation skills can help CEOs deal with the multiplicity of constituent issues. No doubt, delegation is a useful tool to deal with this problem, but it is not a panacea. Successful delegation requires that those to whom tasks are delegated know how to handle these tasks and are credible interacting with the affected groups. For new CEOs, this assumes you can rapidly build a staff well versed in the relevant issues that can "speak for you." This takes time and requires the staff to work closely with the CEO initially to facilitate the learning process, placing even more demands on a new CEO.

Over time, successful delegation can lead to better leverage, but the reality is that for many constituents the CEO has to be "heard" at some point—he has to be in direct communication with various groups. Analysts will accept a CFO's input on guidance and quarterly results, but when it comes to strategy and industry vision the CEO alone must be the primary player. Regulators are comfortable with the general counsel/CFO until the issues become so acute or involve such risk that fiduciary expectations demand the CEO's involvement. Customers may be fine with meeting regularly with business unit heads, but the competitive nature of business often requires that the most senior member of the organization be seen and heard from. Political figures and community leaders are loath to meet with anyone who isn't the CEO, and employee groups and retirees also expect the confirmation that comes when the CEO participates directly. Delegation, therefore, is essential but is not the entire solution.

WAYS TO ADDRESS THE CONSTITUENCIES CONUNDRUM

No simple formula exists for dealing with constituencies. Context differences, varying skills of management teams, the veracity of the issues surrounding the company, the state of play of the industry, and the nature of the concerns of the day all create distinctive complexities. The only thing that's certain in all situations is that CEOs will have too many groups to deal with in a timely fashion.

As confusing and frustrating as this part of the job can be, CEOs can manage their constituencies more effectively if they heed certain lessons.

First, anticipate the overwhelming nature of constituency demands and enter the role knowing that you have to prepare for and expect the onslaught. Have the confidence to segment the needs and set priorities among what look to be equally demanding groups of interested parties. Do rely on others, most notably your general counsel, CFO, and CHRO, to help set priorities and provide leverage.

Second, the challenge isn't just related to finding the time to meet, learn, and discuss but to carve out the time for thinking. The CEO role requires a ton of mental capacity. My clients often complain about how they lack time for real thinking and consideration of tough problems. The challenge isn't scheduling alone but finding significant time with appropriate staff for introspection and reflection. Aspiring CEOs believe they will have this time when they assume leadership, that they finally will be able to take all the inputs from others and make major reasoned decisions. In reality, the whirlwind of constituent management makes this a major challenge. CEOs must find the balance for reflection, and strategic thinking. These are the actions that will most differentiate their success as leaders. Meetings with various constituencies are often important but can detract from the needed effort to re-envision the business.

Third, rapidly build your staff and rely on them. Arrive in a new CEO role with a few trusted lieutenants. You need staff that can anticipate the manner in which you approach problems, speak for you when needed, and act in concert with others to provide leverage and coverage.

Fourth, as a new CEO, establish a standardized approach and processes for managing constituencies quickly. Once advocacy groups know the method by which you wish to interact, they will for the most part, "follow the guideposts." When established protocols and processes are absent, however, those advocating for a point of view get frustrated and seek "end arounds" and shortcuts. Typically, these actions involve press and social media pressure that can turn a potentially well-managed issue into an uncontrolled event.

Fifth, find a grizzled veteran to help prioritize groups and issues. Many organizations employ this type of individual, a veteran executive who is perceptive about and experienced with various stakeholder groups. The person you're searching for is similar to the character featured in old British films, the imperturbable but wise civil servant who helps train neophyte British politicians in the ways of their world. This person can be relied on to tell you that one group is noisy but easily placated, another group has legitimate concerns that must be handled in the coming weeks, and a third group needs to be dealt with immediately or you're going to be subject of an unflattering story on *60 Minutes*. They "get it," and they can help you get it.

Sixth, have a chief of staff. The most effective CEOs I have counseled are those that either have a designated chief of staff or wholly rely on someone on their senior staff to play this role. Some CEOs worry they'll appear too presidential and too hierarchical if they have a chief of staff. Don't let yourself succumb to this fear. Chief of staff doesn't have to be a formal position that serves as your gatekeeper. Rather, most CEOs rotate various employees into this position, using it to find and reward high-talent people within the organization. Whoever assumes this position adds value if and only if they can optimize your time and make the trade-offs necessary to increase your effectiveness. They can and should think about day-to-day as well as and month-to-month and quarter-to-quarter priorities. A chief of staff can also ensure pre-meeting materials are in hand and summarized to ensure productive meetings and can make sure appropriate results and actions are communicated.

IT'S ALL A MATTER OF TIME

Constituency management is a time eater. Given that most CEOs add value to their organizations through their strategic and operational acumen, the more hours devoted to physically meeting with and thinking about constituencies, the less value they can add.

The way constituencies eat away at a CEO's time is insidious. In many instances, it's not one constituency consuming the lion's share of time but a number of them, each taking an increment of hours out of the CEO's week. Years ago, fewer groups existed, so it was easier to manage their demands. Today, this could take the majority of a CEO's time.

Because the proliferation of constituencies is a relatively new phenomenon, CEOs often are ill prepared for the time drain. They didn't hear about this issue when they were in business school; they didn't learn about it when they were rising through the ranks; they never received any training on how to deal with it.

The art of constituency management is practice and learning—learning how to manage constituency demands effectively in the fewest hours possible. The best CEOs develop a management cadence, an instinctive and experiential way of alternating between constituency work and other mission-critical matters.

In this way, they not only have time to do strategic thinking and handle operational issues, but they also have enough hours in the day to reflect, to exercise, and to maintain a healthy perspective.

4

Start Change Management by Changing the Management

The key message from this chapter comes from a piece of wisdom that originated, if memory serves me, with Jack Welch, the legendary former GE CEO. Jack had moved to Boston, and we came to know one another through a series of regular lunches. We shared many stories and reflected on the Boston political landscape with which he became increasingly involved. Jack was a huge Red Sox fan, and while we were watching a game in the middle innings of a less than compelling contest, I turned to him and asked what he thought was the most critical advice he would give to one of my clients who was trying to drive a massive change program. He paused and said, "The best way to ensure successful change management is to start by changing the management."

Don't be fooled by the seemingly simple nature of this advice. My experience tells me that it provides a terrific perspective for leaders to contemplate as they formulate their change strategies. More specifically, it suggests that every CEO should consider:

- How effective "changing the management" can be; and
- The risk/return trade-offs CEOs incur by not changing the management.

The clear priority for a CEO embarking on major shifts is to have the right people in place to make a big change successful. Indeed, the exact nature of a planned change is less important than knowing you have the people to execute the change.

Boards bring in new management to run a company because they seek an increased momentum/speed, as well as greater efficiency and effectiveness of efforts; they also want assurance that the executive team that is executing the changes can be retained and grown so as to sustain the change effort into the future. In so doing, they are assessing the *opportunity cost* of a change management process. Their greatest fear is a process that is over-engineered and becomes bogged down with internal inertia—the momentum for change is undermined, and with it the success of their chosen management leaders. They want to avoid inaction, continued investment in those without adequate skills, and lost time given over to convincing old management to adopt new ways. As Jack Welch so crisply articulated, it is far easier to change out the management rather than try and succeed with under-skilled or change-resistant management.

This same philosophy was in play in the a late 1980s (I wasn't seasoned enough at the time to see it as a key lesson learned until later), when I joined a senior partner and another partner colleague for an initial meeting with Lou Gerstner—he had just begun his tenure as the newly named CEO of RJR Nabisco. Lou had been appointed CEO after the highly publicized battle between different buyout firms for the company. This battle was so public and intense that it became the source material for a bestselling book and a TV movie called *Barbarians at the Gate*.

Lou greeted our senior partner warmly and said, "Thank heavens you are here. I have no one to do any work." When pressed why, Lou said (and I think the following is accurate, though I'm relying on memory of what happened many years ago), "I have been meeting with dozens of executive vice presidents and vice presidents across the business"—which included RJR, Nabisco Foods, Chun King, Associated Biscuits, Walkers UK, Del Monte, and a stake in ESPN—"and I have found few if any of them that adds any value. So I have fired most of them. I got tired of arguing with them about what change was needed." What he needed from us was help launching needed change programs while he recruited new talent.

Gerstner's request embodied Welch's change management approach. It can take too long and require too much effort to convince an existing management team to embrace a new strategic direction and also step up and perform at a higher and more productive level. New management often is simpler, faster, better, and a less risky approach.

Of course, there are many arguments for not being so radical in one's approach. Leaders must be aware of the trade-off: maintaining institutional knowledge in exchange for changing with speed (or vice versa). Opting for speed means some key people will leave, taking away important relationships with key constituents (be they customers, capital sources, equity analysts, suppliers, regulators, etc.). You need to gauge how fast these relationships can be rebuilt with others. Many argue that changing too much management too soon unleashes negative forces throughout the company, with the potential to create fear and even institutional anxiety about the degree of changes being enacted. Others would argue that such "unfreezing of the organizational culture" is a good thing, making it far easier to shift beliefs and behaviors.

Still, changing management is often the best and sometimes the only option for CEOs in challenging situations. While other options may be on the table, they rarely have the impact of bringing in new people with fresh perspectives, innovative ideas, and crucial experience.

Only the most hardened of CEOs are comfortable being seen as uncaring or heartless in the way they deal with underperforming or inherited executives. Indeed, we expect managers and leaders to be empathetic, unlike the more tolerant expectations during the rough and tumble times of Lou Gerstner and Jack Welch. Yet, expectations for results haven't diminished and many would argue that they have increased. This leaves new leaders and CEOs in a catch-22—how do they implement change initiatives aggressively to meet market performance expectations and at the same time be seen as caring and devoted to their management team?

This seems to be a false choice. Typically, only a small number of key leaders need to be replaced. Direct reports to the CEO and members of the C-suite usually number in the 8–12 range—these are usually the core focus for needed changes. Even in today's hyper-transparent, social media–fed PR environment, changes to this group are accepted and rarely get as much notice as one might expect. The new social media environment and the intensity of scrutiny and expectations for CEOs gives them the license to make more shifts in their supporting cast because at the end of the day it is "all about them, less about their team."

The real focus of concern should be on *the entire corporation and its stakeholders*, which is an institutional view. When you shift your focus in this way, the options change significantly: It's now a choice between a possible renewal and re-invigoration of the corporation as opposed to an almost certain slow and steady plateauing and/or decline—brought about by inertia.

Given all the effort that precedes a management change and the positive expectations that the shareholders and the company hope to enjoy as a result of that change, being forceful and action-oriented is crucial. Unfortunately, some new CEOs fall into the trap of being overly cautious and adopting incremental change.

THE ALLURE OF CHANGING SLOWLY—AND THE DANGERS

Many managerial texts support conducting change management in a measured way over time, especially for new CEOs. This consensus suggests working with the company's existing executive team, making adjustments gradually as the styles and abilities of their C-suite teams become known to a recently appointed CEO. For the most part, an evolutionary approach rather than a radical approach is thought best in most circumstances.

No executive likes to begin their time as CEO advocating that large or wholesale change is required for their management team. As noted earlier, many people will question the wisdom of abandoning an existing management team with its institutional knowledge and familiarity with operations and systems, suppliers, and customers. Instead, advocates of keeping the team in place will propose creating a new culture within the existing team. They will argue that new leadership will result in a redirection of effort and with it great returns with less disruption.

Many suggest CEOs analyze the untapped possibilities of their old team and find ways to leverage and redirect and reskill this team. Often they advocate careful and deliberate study, getting to know strengths and weaknesses of individuals as well as analyzing the underlying pace and tone of their team dynamics.

This view requires time—and most organizations don't have time. Effecting operational change requires that executives move quickly. The inertia around change and resistance to adopt new ideas and new approaches should not be underestimated. The fastest way to undermine a change effort is to allow this resistance to gain a solid foothold. The inertia, in other words, can grow to unmanageable proportions in very short timeframes.

Many significant corporate losses can be traced back to inertia. One of the most famous occurred when General

Motors was experiencing a steady decline in the 1980s under the direction of Roger Smith (1981–1990). GM under Smith was facing a daunting situation: a sharp decline in the share of the American market and rising competition from domestic and Japanese companies, whose reputations for quality rose as GM became increasingly associated with making cars of sub-standard quality.

As a response in 1990, the GM board felt they were making a bold move. In contrast to previous trends in choosing company leadership, GM moved away from hiring a new CEO from the ranks of its corporate finance leadership in New York. Instead, they chose Robert Stemple, a classic GM insider who had begun his career in Detroit as an engineer. Unfortunately, Stemple didn't take advantage of the board's initiative by significantly changing the direction of the company. Instead, there was little change in personnel, and many of the changes were resisted by the entrenched management. While there were efforts at improvement, the result was at best small, incremental changes—no "waves" were made when he arrived, and he was ousted two years later, an astonishingly short tenure for a CEO at that time.[1]

But today, things have changed. The response from many boards, consultants, and experienced CEOs is to ignore these conservative approaches to change (such as those pursued by Stemple).

To witness how slow and polite change has been replaced by fast and pragmatic, let's stick with the auto industry. In 2014, Mark Fields ascended from the company ranks as Ford's new CEO, following the relatively successful tenure of Allan Mulally. One of Fields' major initiatives seemed like a safe bet: Expand the sales and global footprint of the Ford Focus through worldwide sourcing for its manufacturing, which would translate into favorable scale effects.

---

[1] http://www.nytimes.com/2011/05/11/business/11stempel.html, http://www.nytimes.com/2007/12/01/business/01smith.html.

Unfortunately for Fields, he and his management team seemed to have not fully anticipated trends that would soon change the car business drastically: hybrid and driverless cars; Tesla and other electric cars; and consumer options that offered popular alternatives to car ownership, such as Uber and Lyft (and ZipCar before them). When these trends undercut Ford's strategy (and lowered the value of Ford's stock drastically), Ford's board of directors replaced him in May of 2017 with somebody from outside the automobile industry, Jim Hacket.

Hacket was the successful CEO of Steelcase, an office furniture company that made its name by finding ways to accommodate the needs of today's tech workers. Hacket's ascent was a sign that technology and mobility had quickly displaced worldwide manufacturing as the source of (traditional) competitive advantage in the car industry. And in a move likely done to make sure that change at Ford was not slowed down by significant internal inertia, Hacket quickly replaced five top executives in the first few weeks of his tenure.[2]

More modern examples abound of new CEOs, after assuming their new roles, quickly making major changes. David Calhoun, after he stepped in as Boeing CEO, elevated Greg Smith to a major role including overseeing enterprise operations, finance and strategy, enterprise services, and corporate administration. Uber CEO Dara Khosrowshahi, following the successful IPO of the company, fired Uber's COO as well as the chief marketing officer. Charles Scharf, the newly named, externally sourced CEO of Wells Fargo, reached out to an alumnus of JP Morgan Chase (where he formerly worked) to become his new COO. He also retired the SVP of bank payments and chief innovation officer and hired another

---

[2] https://www.nytimes.com/2017/05/22/business/ford-ceo-mark-fields-jim-hackett.html, https://www.nytimes.com/2017/05/22/business/jim-hackett-ford.html, http://www.freep.com/story/money/cars/ford/2017/06/18/jim-hackett-ford-design/399048001/.

JP Morgan Chase alumnus to be head of cards, retail, and merchant services.

Such stories of management changes appear almost daily; it has become the norm that CEOs seeking to initiate change begin by assembling a new and loyal team.

THE NEED TO MAKE THE MOST OF TWO VERY SCARCE RESOURCES: TIME AND TRUST

A change in the leadership of a company usually happens when things are going badly, not when they are going well. This means that two things that are necessary for a corporation to work at peak performance—time and trust—are in short supply. If the corporation is facing reductions in revenues or new, worrisome threats from competition, then time is short. If the executive team is not leading the company or an activist is in the wings, then trust in leadership is being reduced as well.

At this point, most employees and other stakeholders are nervous about the future and tired of losing in the present. They're eager, in fact, to be led by people who won't be wasting their time and undercutting their trust. Quick to see that slow, conservative management has not been effective, many employees in an underperforming firm will be *eager* to be led by competent management. After months or maybe even years of working in a phlegmatic, risk-avoidant underperforming culture, they want to move ahead in a bolder direction. Given a fresh, bold approach, CEOs can release all sorts of positive, pent-up energy. They're revved up by a strategy that makes sense and management that is committed to making it work quickly. Employees start going to work with a new spring in their step—instead of dragging their feet.

Over the years, I've witnessed the effects of fast and decisive change management strategies and how they help achieve ambitious goals. Some of these change efforts were dramatic and decisive; others were quieter and subtler (but powerful and quick-acting in their own way). Although the leaders featured in the following two case studies replaced their existing executive teams, they tailored their change strategies to suit their particular situations.

SUCCESSFULLY TRANSITIONING AFTER A MERGER OR ACQUISITION: AMERICAN AIRLINES

In 2013 the CEO of US Airways, Doug Parker, orchestrated a daring move to acquire American Airlines. This was a case of a "minnow" eating the "whale"—the minnow being the #5 airline with $14 billion in annual revenues, and the whale being the #3 airline with $42 billion. At the time of the acquisition, American was emerging from bankruptcy and was highly vulnerable. US Airways swooped in with promises for better outcomes for the influential unions and a compliant creditor committee, and US Airways and Doug Parker carried the day.

After the purchase came the next significant decision— would this be a merger or a takeover? More specific to our point here: Would change management be enacted by replacing key executives or through a blending of the two management teams? In 2005, Parker had been CEO of America West when that airline bought the larger US Airways. In that case, Parker relied on the existing America West executive team to take charge of the new entity that was created by the merger.

He decided to use the same change management approach again. As incoming CEO of American Airlines in 2015, Parker chose to rely on the team he brought in from America West to run US Airways. Five senior colleagues occupied the roles of leaders of operations, finance, sales and marketing, human resources, and corporate affairs and public affairs. By 2013, the group of six had known each other for years and had developed a high degree of trust and confidence in one another. Now COO, Robert Isom, noted that this team was unusually close: "Ours is not a traditional CEO to senior team relationship; it is more informal and more familial."

But despite the strength of the US Airways team, could changing the management team at American work given the huge size difference between the two companies? Moreover, the two company cultures were quite different, with American Airlines being a "marketing-driven entity" focusing on customer service while US Airways was much more concerned with operational efficiency.

Parker had decided early on that this was going to be a takeover in terms of the executive management team. The far broader effort of integration had many elements of a merger since many other systems, processes, and other organizational levels were brought together in a collective fashion. The executive teams, though, could not be merged. Time was the crucial factor. The time—and the concomitant effort and expense—for a true integration of the two senior management teams would have meant delay and inertia. Parker firmly signaled his intentions by announcing in early 2013 that while the headquarters for the new merged airline would be Dallas (American Airline's HQ location) and not Phoenix (where US Airways was based) he and his whole senior management team would be moving to Dallas and leading the combined airline and that much of the old American senior executive team would not be needed.

Parker, by bringing his core senior leadership team with him from US Airways to head the new company, didn't have to waste time creating a change mentality among his senior team. He needed a team that was motivated and capable of driving massive change. He trusted his team to speak honestly and objectively about all the changes that needed to be implemented, and he required this straight talk about tough issues right from the start.

Second, Parker was aware that if he only relied exclusively on his management team from US Airways, he might be poorly perceived by American employees, and they would resist his changes. For this reason, he appointed three key American executives to key positions. He chose American's CIO to head the combined airlines systems and technology platforms—an incredibly important job at an airline. In addition, he retained American's Chief Restructuring Officer/Treasurer even though there was no Treasury job for her. Instead, he appointed the former American CRO to a new position of Chief Integration Officer, charged with running the integration of the two companies. Parker also retained American's former Government Relations Officer. With these appointments, Parker sent the message to everyone that the team he felt was best suited to meet his needs and that of the newly combined airline was now in place.

Third, by changing the senior management team so aggressively and so weighted toward the US Airways executives, Parker created an environment in which everything was up for discussion. It was clear that some of the old ways of American were soon going to be behind them.

Changing the management need not be dramatic or abrupt to be effective. Harvard University's past president, Drew Faust, quietly changed the deans at all of the major schools (law, business, faculty of arts and sciences, etc.) when she took over as president of the University in 2007. She described her leadership style this way: "I … think that you can be very tough and very gentle at the same time, that being tough doesn't mean being noisy or cruel or aggressive, it just means standing your ground and pursuing your goals and being equitable and decent to people."

Faust became president of Harvard on the heels of the short-lived presidency of Larry Summers, who lasted as Harvard's president for only five years, after his tenure was truncated by several controversial moves that he had made and comments he had said. Although Summers' style was brash, many of his plans for the future of the university were to some degree adopted and further enhanced by Faust.

One of the most well-known parts of Summers' vision was to better integrate Harvard's many schools. Under Faust, the initiative became known as "One Harvard" in 2011. But unlike Summers, Faust made these changes largely under the radar, installing deans who shared her vision of encouraging collaborative research and academic offerings across campus—and she did this quickly. One of her appointees, the Dean of Arts and Sciences Michael Smith, vocally supported Faust's "One Harvard" vision: "One of the things we want to do here is not just push forward with individual basic research in the sciences and engineering, but also have connections made with the professional schools."

Traditionally, Harvard's 12 schools have pursued their respective goals in isolation, what has become known as the "every tub on its own bottom" approach. Given that the strong independence of the schools has been cultivated for years, the incentive to "change the management" at the university seems quite logical and useful. The lasting success of Faust's move to change the management can probably only be assessed after the passage of many years, but her first steps toward this direction were as decisive as they were tactful. Upon her retirement in 2018 she was met with near universal approval and admiration of all of Harvard University's stakeholders.

CHANGE REQUIRES EMPATHY, CLARITY, AND COURAGE

If change management requires changing the management, this does not mean losing empathy for others or making a big show of things just to make a statement. As Drew Faust demonstrated, a new leader can make changes without having to create drama. And, as Faust also demonstrated, the key ingredient for seeing a change program through to its completion is standing your ground as you enact the changes you believe are necessary. Faust was modest enough to continue some of the major goals of a predecessor who had left under controversial circumstances because she believed in the idea of creating "One Harvard." Once she adopted that goal, she enacted her changes with both subtlety and determination.

Faust, like any new successful CEO, was clear and confident about the goals she was striving for. Arriving in the job deeply and widely prepared—qualities we discussed earlier—was crucial. With preparation comes clarity, and with clarity comes the courage to stick to your plans when they meet with resistance. Even more important than clarity is the confidence in creating an executive team you can trust with the ambitious objective of major change.

More specifically, here are three ways CEOs can exhibit these crucial qualities:

1. **Empathy.** By demonstrating a commitment to the long-term viability of the institution, you show that you're in tune with the concerns of employees. Empathy isn't about being "soft"—about expressing how much you care about people. These are often just words, and employees may view them cynically. At American, Doug Parker created empathy by demonstrating his willingness to do everything possible to preserve the airline—to take whatever actions were necessary for the greater good of the majority of employees. People "got" that he cared deeply about the institution—that he cared for the enterprise that kept them all employed at a company they loved. Empathy also is a counterbalance to survivor's guilt. During some change programs, people lose their jobs. In mergers/acquisitions, duplicate roles often exist (two CFOs, two CMOs, etc.), and in many cases only one of them will be retained. By being empathic—by making sure that the person who is let go is treated fairly—you are more likely to get buy-in from the people who remain.

2. **Clarity.** CEOs who contradict themselves or are ambiguous can cripple their change efforts. To be clear, leaders need to hold to their principles. By not wavering from them, they demonstrate what they stand for and how committed they are to their beliefs. Too often, CEOs embarking on change management strategies say one thing and do another. As a result, stakeholders begin to lose their faith in leadership. In addition, consistency is a close cousin of clarity. By acting on principles over

time and in a variety of situations, people get a sense of who you are and what is meaningful to you. You aren't just a reactive CEO but one who operates from a strong foundation.

3. **Courage.** Expect pushback as the leader of change, and when you get it, you need to show the courage of your convictions. The pushback can be from all sorts of groups—employees, unions, consumer advocacy groups, investors, boards. I serve on a board, and the company recently made a significant acquisition of an organization that does a lot of government work. As part of the deal's financials and the transaction's underlying plan was the need to downsize about 2000 employees. When meeting with the CEO, one of the board members confronted him and asked, "Do we really have to get rid of that many people?" This board member didn't want to be seen as mean-spirited, and he was pushing hard for the CEO to come up with another solution to the cost problems that came with the acquisition. To his credit, the CEO didn't back down. Instead, he insisted that if they wanted to produce products that met government specifications/cost requirements, they had no choice but to eliminate the positions. Change often rubs people the wrong way and involves choices with which not everyone agrees. CEOs who are brave enough to make these choices despite opposition are the ones most likely to lead successful change initiatives.

5

Avoid Becoming Isolated

The irony of being CEO is that you're surrounded by large numbers of staff, executives, employees, and interested outsiders, yet many CEOs feel isolated. New CEOs say to me one of the most surprising aspects of finally being such a leader is the accompanying sense of being alone. Certainly, there is no shortage of demand on a leader's time and attention. Most say that there are few moments without a steady stream of communications, both electronic and face-to-face. There's always someone who wants something. Scheduled meetings, lunches, conferences, and talks dominate their calendar, and phone calls, emails and texts are constant, yet the sense of isolation comes from the absence of people around them without agendas and lacking vested interest. CEOs, like other executives, need trusted colleagues and peers to whom they can turn. During my CEO interviews for this book, many leaders said something to the effect that in the end, "you occupy the position alone."

This sense of isolation is compounded by the fact that in previous positions, theses leaders sensed they were an integral part of a managerial team. Psychologically, being the leader is an isolating job. You're under intense scrutiny from all sides: from executives, from employees (below), from your board (above), and from customers, shareholders, and other stakeholders (the side). No longer is there someone above you to turn to for help, counsel, or at least understanding and empathy. Most feel like they can't show weakness or express uncertainty, fear, or frustration. They have to be a strong, confident leader on the outside who shows fortitude and strength (even when they might not always feel this way).

On the inside, though, you are lonely at the top, and this can be a counterproductive mindset for a CEO. The good news is that this mindset isn't a given, and CEOs possess the ability to avoid isolation and feel more connected.

HOW ISOLATION HAPPENS

CEOs can feel alone during any part of their tenure, but the sense of being solitary often is most acute when they arrive in the job. Consider the genesis of this lonely feeling.

A corporation greets a new CEO with much anticipation and high expectations—usually hoping that previous leadership challenges and missteps will be addressed and that the trajectory of the business will finally be pointing upward. Yet these leadership changes are also met with anxiety by all involved: by the board, who will have their choice questioned; by the outgoing CEO, who worries about his or her legacy; by the senior staff, who wonders whether the new CEO will keep the team intact; by employees, who wonder what changes are coming; and by analysts and outside stakeholders, who want to see a new trajectory. A new CEO portends new directions, new priorities, and new ways of doing things. Executives and employees know that how they adjust to these changes coming from the CEO and the C-suite could make or break their careers. Everyone tries to read the CEO very carefully to present themselves in the best light possible.

Given this environment, CEOs often find themselves in very uncomfortable situations, facing unique communications and information challenges that they have likely never faced before. First, CEOs, particularly those promoted from within, learn that the executives and staff they used to turn to for help within the corporation are no longer as forthcoming or candid as they used to be. As a result, fewer people exist who the CEO can trust as confidants as well as fewer opportunities to hear honest feedback. Second, when CEOs lack confidants and honest feedback, they encounter more risks, since they know less about the corporation and its issues than they should. These two challenges combined often result in a new (and often unanticipated) state of isolation that increases emotional distance and stress for the new leader.

Unlike the more analyzable issues such as need for more organic revenue or a technological upgrade, these situations are subtle, making them difficult to recognize and correct. CEOs who wished they knew more about their companies may unknowingly wall themselves off.

Ascending to a powerful leadership position puts many CEOs in a novel role for which they're not often psychologically prepared. This lack of preparation, in turn, often puts them on the defensive, which can be a position of weakness. So instead of tending to the communication problems that could improve their leadership and their sense of connection, they often get stuck in their initial emotional discomfort. Their defensive reactions to unhappy news and difficult feedback may make them feel better in the short run—because they create the illusion that they're in control—but it only worsens the already delicate personal relationships they need to maintain if they are to lead their companies successfully.

On top of all this, most people aren't prepared for the speed and intensity with which things change. Cognitively, CEOs get it—they recognize that becoming the head of the company will alter their relationships and affect their daily routines. But they assume that the transition to CEO will be like previous promotions to leadership roles of greater responsibility and authority.

As a result, they are unprepared for how quickly and radically their work environment changes. They are surprised that the colleagues who used to stop by their office routinely to chat no longer do. The hierarchical nature of companies (and despite the recent trend in structural flattening of companies, hierarchies persist) ensures that whoever is "top of the house" will often be there by themselves.

Contrary to what you might expect, this sense of isolation is more intense if you're promoted into the job from the inside rather than if you arrive from the outside. As an outsider, your expectations are more aligned with reality; you recognize that you're coming to a company where you know few people and have few allies. Consequently, you're a bit better prepared for the loneliness of the job. As someone who has been promoted to the position internally, though, you are surrounded by familiar faces. Like a thirsty sailor on the ocean, water is everywhere, but there's not a drop to drink. You have trouble processing how all your relationships have changed.

CREATING YOUR OWN SHELL

Some CEOs make a bad situation worse by erecting barriers to honest and open communication. They often don't realize that they're isolating themselves because of their behaviors, but the effect can quickly result in discouraging people from sharing bad news or challenging their positions.

Eduardo, for instance, had been the CEO of a large company for four years, and he was a formidable presence. Large and imposing physically, with a loud booming voice, Eduardo intimidated people without intending to do so. Not only was Eduardo smart and accomplished—he'd been successful in two previous senior BU leadership roles—but he was also aggressive and commanding in his manner. In his current CEO position, his senior team feared him. Each of them had seen or borne the brunt of his harsh criticisms.

While Eduardo's executive coach had given him feedback about how intimidating he could be, Eduardo rationalized it. Eduardo believed that his door was always open, that people viewed him as a "good guy," and that his people felt free to say whatever they wanted to him. Eduardo liked to think of himself as a strong leader and was in denial about how that strength effectively shut him off from information and ideas. He might talk to a lot of people during the course of the day, but he was isolated figuratively, removed from opinions that differed from his, and from negative news that others judged might cause him to become angry.

Anthony is another CEO who took actions that isolated him. After a few months of heading his company, he selected Larry for a major C-suite role. Larry was a top executive with a sterling track record who was known to be willing to speak her mind. Ostensibly, Larry's forthrightness was one of the reasons Anthony hired him. Anthony gave him a position of great responsibility in the company and welcomed his straight talk—he used him as a sounding board for his initiatives and valued his willingness to tell him exactly what he thought of them. For a while, things went well, but then Larry started emailing direct reports about his disagreements with Anthony to Jill. In his emails, he recounted some of his debates with Anthony about various policies and how disappointed he was about the lack of action Anthony was taking. Larry believed he erred too often on the side of caution and that company would be better off if he were to "show more guts." Anthony learned of the emails and fired Larry immediately. No doubt, Larry made a mistake by complaining to a subordinate about Anthony (and worsened the error by doing so in a communication medium that wasn't secure). Nonetheless, Anthony's decision to fire him sent a signal to the rest of his team. He was communicating that he didn't like being contradicted or disagreed with. Anthony could feel justified in his actions, but the effect of his actions was to signal that dissent would not be welcomed. Once Larry was removed, any member of his team who disagreed with Anthony now would think twice before verbalizing that disagreement. Though Anthony met with and talked to a lot of people in his company, he was further isolated from dissenting opinions and disagreeable news.

In the past, Eduardos and Anthonys were more the norm—rugged individualists who relish being atop organizations and going it alone. For example, Dennis Picard of Raytheon and Rand Araskog of ITT are just two of several CEOs with whom I have worked who were well known for being tough, no-nonsense leaders who were more command-and-control than collaborative. Today, this leadership mindset has changed, and we're seeing more leaders who are willing to engage with others, welcome diverse opinions, and share the spotlight. Still, isolationism remains a significant problem. Even leaders who demonstrate a willingness to connect with others are vulnerable to backsliding, however. What often happens is that CEOs are collaborative for a period of time but then make a decision where there are winners and losers. The losers are upset, CEOs regret allowing others to participate in the decision-making, and respond to that upset by withdrawing from the collaborative process.

TRANSITIONING TO A GOOD COMMUNICATIONS REGIME

The New Communications Landscape for Newly Tenured Leaders

The saying "It's lonely at the top" feels like an apt description to many CEOs looking back at their tenure, but it doesn't have to be that way. This state of isolation for CEOs often comes *after* making a series of crucial mistakes; they are avoidable mistakes, rooted in poor communication and a sense of defensiveness.

While the consequences of bad communication between the CEO and the rest of the corporation are significant, they also are subtle in the way they create isolation. To explore these subtleties, I'll use two hypothetical situations, one with a CEO who finds productive ways to share information with his staff (called "Anderson") and another with a CEO who does not (called "Jacobs").

In the beginning, the stories of both CEO Anderson and Jacobs are practically the same. Before becoming CEOs, they had demonstrated great managerial skills. Not only could they lead discrete teams well, but they also led multiple teams within a company hierarchy.

When they ascend to the role of CEO, though, Anderson and Jacobs encounter problems with former peers: There is little sharing of office politics, and more prepackaged information generally with a positive outlook or spin. Meetings adjourn without the informal and productive hallway follow-ups with colleagues, people agree with them much more often than they used to, and requests for honest feedback from subordinates very rarely lead to ideas or input that might challenge (implicitly or explicitly) their point of view.

For both Anderson and Jacobs, this new situation was shocking. Before becoming CEOs, both of them had shared a lot of information with their colleagues. Then, they found themselves with all of that communication infrastructure below them—and, ironically, largely out of their reach (even though they had become the most powerful person in their respective corporations). They had ascended to their leadership role assuming that all the communication and camaraderie that had been part of their success would continue. But now as leaders, they find themselves cut off from the ideas and information that previously had flowed freely. They know that they require more information and debate to inform their high-stakes decisions, but they don't know how to access it. It's not that no one talks to them or provides them with ideas and information; it's that the flow is filtered and formalized, and it makes them feel like a screen that allows little to pass thought it has been erected between themselves and their people.

Although the cause of this isolation can vary from company to company, one organizational factor often contributes to the seclusion of the CEO: putting this leader on a pedestal. Many people tend to treat company leaders as somehow above it all, as secular kings/queens within the organizational realm. And while their accomplishments at times may be described as exceptional, CEOs are flawed humans like the rest of us. When colleagues fail to recognize their leader's fundamental humanity (with its strengths and especially its weaknesses), they help create the first and most fundamental barrier of communication between CEOs and their stakeholders.

CEOs might be fully aware of their isolation or they may only react to it instinctively (without consciously recognizing how isolated they are). In either case, there are choices they make to deal with this situation, some better and some worse. Once CEOs make these choices, their decisions tend to shape communication patterns. Because CEOs' actions often cascade quickly through the organization, early signs of how the CEO wants to communicate can become habits and rules of thumb almost overnight.

Like most incoming CEOs, Jacobs was brought in during a time of distress for his company; they had just completed a major acquisition a little more than 12 months before, and the integration of the new company was going poorly. Jacobs wasn't sure whether a misalignment of the two companies' respective strengths was the problem, the culprit was cultural differences, or an unidentified external issue was exacerbating the situation.

After a month on the job, Jacobs was growing desperate, since solutions to the problem of underperformance remained elusive. Jacobs was surprised to hear that a few prominent analysts were spreading doubt about his leadership style after such a short period of time. They used words such as "tepid" and "indecisive" to characterize his style—words that no one had ever used to describe him before. He couldn't understand why he was under such intense and negative scrutiny at such an early stage. The company stock had dipped just a few days after his ascension, but it didn't seem significant enough to call him "tepid." What was going wrong?

Jacobs began to feel fearful about the future and reacted to this fear in ways that only made his search for answers more difficult. Instead of seeking alternative ways to obtain more salient information about his company, Jacobs found ways to mask his uncertainty about the future. To do this, he minimized his chances of encountering "the unexpected": To hide any doubt he had in his own abilities, Jacobs asked a minimum of open-ended questions of his colleagues and rarely requested opinions on broad topics. Instead of trying to develop relationships with other executives on a one-to-one basis to encourage openness and dialogue, Jacobs tried to convey "strength" and "fairness" by treating everybody exactly the same way. And despite his disdain for leaders who seemed to love to feed their own egos, Jacobs managed to surround himself with a few "yes-like" staff (even though Jacobs did not recognize them as such). In contrast to the views of most of the executive team, Jacobs saw these "yes-like" staff as among the smarter people in the company.

Compensating for the Potential Loneliness of the New CEO Landscape: Anderson

CEO Anderson faced a very similar situation to CEO Jacobs, but she recognized her growing isolation and took steps to minimize it. Anderson understood that the problems facing the corporation were far too complex to micromanage; Anderson also recognized that her fear of failure might cause her to dictate rather than invite frank conversations and that she might micromanage out of fear rather than engage with an open mind. She came to realize that she couldn't be successful alone and was determined to create communications habits around the office and among her staff that would allow her to receive the best help available from the talent around her.

Although Anderson was not averse to hearing criticism even when stressed, she was caught up in the new problems and challenges of her role. She didn't realize at first that she was sending a signal to others that she was "too busy" to engage. But when she noticed her conversations with executives were often short and lacked a lot of "context" around the numeric and factual information being shared, she decided to change this dynamic. To allow her executive team an opportunity to openly exchange their ideas and get to know her, Anderson made it a priority to slow down to chat with individual members of her team on a regular, one-on-one basis—outside of her office. This was a conscious act; she made it a priority and undertook a deliberate effort to engage more actively in these conversations. Anderson wanted to get to know how each executive liked to communicate and interact, which would take some patience and persistence on her part. Although this was a labor-intensive goal, Anderson believed it would pay off in the long run.

During these one-on-one conversations, Anderson listened and asked a lot of questions of each executive. The questions reflected not only respect for an executive's expertise, but they also revealed some of Anderson's humility. She was frank about aspects of the business she didn't know well and conveyed a sincere desire to learn from her staff. After some weeks of these one-on-one conversations, executives did not see Anderson as aloof and unapproachable. Instead, her requests for help encouraged them to share information even when she didn't ask them directly for it. Their comfort level grew as they learned that they did not have to be perfect, either.

CONNECTING WITH BOARDS

Communication habits adopted by CEOs with direct reports tend to be repeated across the corporation, including the board of directors. As a result, CEOs may not only be distanced from their teams and employees but from their boards as well. Recognize that boards provide opportunities for honest conversation, inclusion, and connection—opportunities that may be more natural with boards than those involving subordinates. Even if a CEO thinks there's a free flow of information between him and his subordinates, his position of superiority in the corporation creates an imbalance of power that tends to discourage employees from always being frank. Within the boardroom, in contrast, the CEO can be first among equals—a leader surrounded by peers who have comparable talent and achievements. They can provide both the experience *and* candor that CEOs truly need. More than that, they can make CEOs feel like they're part of a team, providing the straight talk and empathic ear that foster feelings of affiliation and inclusion.

When CEOs struggle to establish strong lines of communication with the rest of the company, creating bonds with boards is an imperative. CEOs require people in whom they can confide and from whom they can receive honest feedback. Without a supportive board of directors, CEOs are not only unaware of many of the realities being faced by the business, but they can also be doubted and sometimes undercut by the board. As a result, no safe refuge exists for CEOs within their own companies, and their stress levels and sense of isolation increase.

REACH OUT TO THE RIGHT PEOPLE

Beyond all the isolating factors we've discussed, CEOs are often walled off from other people because of the type of work that comes with the job. Being CEO involves grappling with a never-ending stream of strategic, operational, legal, and regulatory issues. The legal and regulatory challenges are the ones that are often the most vexing for CEOs because of the volume of these issues and the difficulty of resolving them. Years ago, these issues also existed, but they were fewer in number and less difficult to resolve. Today, it can be an employee filing a sexual harassment suit one day and a government agency filing an injunction against the company the next. There are a web of tax issues, political matters to consider, and government bureaucracies to navigate.

CEOs can be consumed by all these demands. They often seem like they're in crisis mode, which leaves less time for handling critical operational and organizational issues. The regimen of reporting and oversight is daunting now and will become even more so in the future. Leaders could easily spend most of their time dealing with the legal and regulatory demands, and when they do, they develop a siege mentality.

For this reason, CEOs should make general counsels and CFOs their best friends. Two of my former McKinsey alums, Dominic Casserley of Willis Insurance and Michael P. Fox of Stroz Friedberg, swore by their general counsels once they became CEOs; they were quick to praise these colleagues as providing the type of guidance and assistance that made dealing with myriad regulations tolerable. More to the point, their general counsels helped them realize that they were not alone. Similarly, trusted CFOs are invaluable since they are the ones who can both interpret the numbers and deal with the myriad of financial analysts, shareholders, and regulatory oversight, as well as capital sources and rating agencies.

Exacerbating the isolation is the sense of weight on a CEO's shoulders. It's not just the work or the tough decisions, but the sheer mental and physical exhaustion that comes with the territory. It's a cliché to call any job 24/7, but CEOs are always on call, and their calendars are optimized so they lack the downtime necessary to take a moment and reflect.

Many of the CEOs interviewed for this book spoke of the loss of time for long, leisurely lunches with colleagues where the discussions roam where they might. Gone too are the hours when you could contemplate an issue in a relaxed, unpressured manner, where you could allow the minutes to tick by without other matters intruding.

From a physical standpoint, many interviewed noted how tough it was to stay in shape—there's not enough time to work out regularly, and the mental exhaustion makes it tough to summon the energy to go to the gym. The travel is constant and unrelenting, and sometimes it feels like you're spending more time on the plane than anywhere else.

Perhaps the best way to capture the demands of the job is by describing what it's like to be in a meeting. In the past as a non-CEO you attended meetings, but you didn't have to be "on" all the time. You were not the centerpiece of every meeting, and even when you were, you could let others take center stage. As CEO, though, every eye is on you. Everyone is attuned not only to what you say but also to the expression on your face, your body language, the tone of your voice, and your overall mood. After many such meetings of being ultra-attentive, it gets exhausting.

Everyone wants something from you. I remember John Watson, CEO of Chevron-Texaco, saying how he didn't have control of his calendar and even worse, how he was surprised by how much the job affected him and his own self-image. John, who always took pride in being in good shape, said it wasn't just that he couldn't work out when he wanted, but that he was like a pawn in someone else's game, being moved from meeting to meeting, city to city, group to group.

John recalled that when oil was at $100 a barrel, he was a hero, but when it dropped to $30, he was in trouble. He said that every activist, shareholder group, and employee group was yelling because the stock dropped. "I can't change that, but they think I should. It was very hard to remember that I wasn't a genius when the stock was high because of the macro oil market and I wasn't an idiot when price of oil drove the stock to new lows."

A new CEO once said to me, "Imagine you have a video camera filming you 24/7 and streaming what you do, what you say, and how you say it. It's taxing."

All of this contributes to a sense of not being in control, and that's a lonely feeling. One way to counteract this is for CEOs to have a trusted confidante—someone who is concerned about the CEO's mental and physical health—who is trustworthy, who can listen as well as offer advice. It could be a spouse or a best friend. Some leaders develop "kitchen cabinets," unofficial advisors who may be former colleagues, mentors, and so on. Still others are fortunate enough to form a bond with a board member. It really doesn't matter who it is, as long as there is someone CEOs can rely on to relieve the isolation of the job.

FIVE WAYS TO KEEP CONNECTED

CEOs can slip into an isolated default mode without realizing it. Because they're so busy and often surrounded by people, it feels as if they're engaged and involved. Similarly, CEOs receive a stream of communication from a variety of sources, so they may not realize that they're filtering out information they don't want to hear by intimidating or ignoring people. And they may not admit to themselves or others how lonely or mentally exhausting the job is and try to "tough it out," refusing to seek help from people they trust.

As the previous section suggested, finding a confidante and making the company's general counsel your best friend are two ways to counteract the isolating effects of the job. Here are five other steps you can take:

1. **Fight your denial reflex.** This is especially difficult if you're a strong, authoritative leader who is reluctant to show weakness. It's easier to soldier on and pretend you're feeling no pain. Over time, though, CEOs pay a price for denial. They become more and more isolated, and eventually it takes a toll. Better to admit that you're feeling drained and lonely and finding a way to manage these feelings.

2. **Get off the pedestal.** As CEO, people treat you differently than others; they are more reluctant to speak their minds, to tell you bad news, to disagree with your ideas. Communicate by word and deed that you're open to all input. It's not enough to say you want to hear bad news or that your door is always open. You really have to mean it and behave in a way that is consistent with these messages.

3. **Communicate the importance of connectivity to your team.** Make it clear to everyone in the C-suite that you expect openness, honesty, and trusting relationships not only of yourself but also of them—that these are shared requirements. Your people will mirror your behaviors, so recognize the value of modeling connective attitudes and actions.

4. **Avoid recidivism.** I've watched CEOs make efforts to connect for periods of time, but they then slip back into old, isolationist patterns. They don't do this consciously, but if they've been traditional command-and-control leaders for many years and have been practicing connective behaviors for only a short time, they can become recidivists because of that long history. Be vigilant against returning to old habits.

5. **Have the "best ears in the company."** Here's a story that explains this last piece of advice. Bill Russell was one of the greatest players in NBA history when he played for the Boston Celtics, and his coach was the legendary Red Auerbach. In an interview with Russell, he talked about his coach and how he never really "played" for Red, since they "worked together" as a team. Russell recalled that Red would have conversations with each player, but that he tailored his style of communication to the needs of each. Despite the variation in styles, his goal was to hear what each player needed and adjust his coaching accordingly. Russell said that Red had "the best ears in the NBA." Becoming a brilliant listener may not seem like a typical leadership requirement, but it is essential to form connections with people.

Ask yourself: Do I have the best ears in my company? If not, you need to try harder to develop this ability. By listening, you can ensure that you engage others, get the real truth, and connect more relationally; it also will help you fight the insularity and sense of isolationism that comes with leadership roles.

6

Manage the Mentorship Conundrum

To mentor or not to mentor, that often seems to be the question. While it's not a question that CEOs would publicly ask (and possibly not even acknowledge to themselves), it's one that affects their performance as CEO, their relationship with the board, and the legacy they leave.

You won't find any CEOs who say, "I don't believe in mentoring my direct reports." But you will find CEOs who avoid becoming a true mentor because it's hard to do well, takes a lot of time, and is not always directly related to their immediate performance challenges. In addition, there's the psychological challenge: They realize they are being asked to identify, train, and promote their own replacement. While CEOs will acknowledge that this is their role, their actions may not be consistent with this role—it's challenging to prepare someone to replace them.

As a result of the challenge to mentor actively and the need to acknowledge that they're not essential, some CEOs fail to make the consistent and sustained efforts required to develop successors. This puts the board in a challenging position. Without a skilled CEO replacement, boards have one of three choices when they feel the need to address CEO leadership: Stick with the existing CEO and hope for a change in performance; promote from within, knowing that the selected candidate will be knowledgeable about the company but possibly not fully ready; or take the added risk of going outside for new leadership. Not only does this leave companies scrambling for options when CEOs fail, but these organizations also often don't establish a culture of mentorship—a culture that is critical in today's challenging environment.

A GROWING NEED IN ORGANIZATIONS

As the pace of change and the challenge of the global economy increases, the need for effective, long-term, corporate-enabled mentorship activity becomes ever greater. Mentorship contributes to the healthy development of younger executives as well as the shaping of an agile business culture—both of which are crucially important in dealing with demands of an ever-shifting, dynamic economic environment.

In the command-and-control past, mentorship was less important because senior executives tended to be directive, and senior staff was informed as to what was expected of them. With a bit of coaching and a great deal of performance pressure, employees would respond positively, and learning was more experiential. Today, the demands of the market and the expectations of employees at all levels require greater development initiative, an embrace of learning, and a pursuit of personal growth and developmental learning opportunities. Mentors facilitate these activities. They are able to offer guidance and support as well as help individuals secure growth-targeted assignments. Unlike traditional top-down-minded executives, mentors play a number of different roles that are critical in today's flattened organizations—they are coaches, teachers, confidants, and "life influencers."

Executing mentorship well requires a considerable commitment from both companies and individuals. This is especially true as companies increasingly have to rely on organizations that produce cross-functional team environments. Companies often deal with unexpected challenges when employing teams composed of people from across the organization with both functional and line responsibilities. For instance, departments concerned with marketing, technology, and IT often work closely with a variety of business units across a corporation, especially when a new product or service is going to market. This cross-fertilization happens repeatedly, and it requires people to cooperate, communicate, and learn across business functions and business units. The resulting organizational structure is universally recognized as one of many variations on a "matrix"—a flexible and powerful configuration of employees that adds complexity.

Experienced senior executives at the top of the company or the leaders of a major business unit will have developed (out of necessity) the skills to navigate this kind of organizational structure. But if an enterprise is going to be successful, everybody has to learn how to work in a matrix that is constantly adapting and in motion—similar to the flow of play on a soccer field or a basketball court. In sports, coaches facilitate team play. In organizations, mentors play a key role in helping employees develop the same artistry and necessary flexibility of performance.

To help people attain significant agility, a successful company needs to develop a "we" culture (instead of an "I" culture), where the success of the team or the company takes precedence over the individual star. Or, to look at it another way, sometimes a particular employee will become the "star" of a big project; at other times, that same employee will act in a supporting role. In either case, an employee's overall "success" at his or her job is not judged by individual achievement alone but rather by how many successful projects participated in—as well as the respect that has been earned from colleagues.

MENTORSHIP ROLES AND RESPONSIBILITIES

To create and maintain an agile "we" culture, organizations must embrace mentorship—a process that develops individual talent on a one-to-one basis. Unfortunately, many organizations put much more emphasis on shaping their employees through formal training programs that take place in classrooms or at off-site retreats. As some compelling academic research has shown, completion of these training programs is often not very effective in the long run. Training sessions can be useful for networking and building coalitions within a company and often have a positive networking and reward component to them. But they are not necessarily able to build the skills and train executives to work collaboratively.

The vast majority of learning at a company actually comes from "learning by doing" *and* "by doing together." During my career at McKinsey, it was a common belief among my colleagues that 80 percent of what we learned was derived from working with teammates, clients, and partners. But effective learning doesn't happen just by throwing different kinds of people together in a joint effort. Mentors help employees understand what they need to learn, when they need to learn it, and how to integrate what they have learned into their day-to-day responsibilities.

The best mentors focus on three elements related to their mentees' careers: coaching (in its traditional sense), career guidance, and sponsorship. Coaching helps employees deal with change over time—from the nuts and bolts of a new position to, more importantly, understanding how to assume new leadership responsibilities. In the career guidance role, mentors help younger employees recognize the trade-offs between personal and professional goals and responsibilities, their relationship to the corporate entity, and decisions they have to make for the immediate future as well as the long term. Finally, mentees benefit immensely from sponsorship. Employees with great potential can make some big mistakes or miss some promising opportunities in the early stages of their careers. In a sponsorship role, mentors can provide crucial assistance by standing up and assuring others that their mentees can be trusted to accomplish a particular task and are worth the further investment and patience that is often required to develop great talent.

At McKinsey, mentorship effects were highly visible. Senior partners knew who was mentoring and supporting other colleagues. The support of others was visible, and it was accepted that one was "brought along" with the help of more senior members of the firm. A successful mentorship creates a rewarding relationship for both parties concerned, and the resulting bonds of understanding and affection can last a lifetime.

BOARD EXPECTATIONS, CEO RESISTANCE

When CEOs model mentorship behaviors, their actions cascade throughout the organization. They send a clear message that mentorship is an actionable priority, not merely something that they give lip service to but fail to translate into behaviors. As important as it is for CEOs to launch and support formal mentorship programs, their biggest contribution is taking mentorship actions relative to successors.

And this can be a tough thing for CEOs to do. Instead, some rationalize and prevaricate, at times avoiding taking this responsibility as seriously as might be needed. I've heard CEOs tell their boards that time will solve the problem of no candidate having sufficient experience (to replace the CEO) and argue for patience and further development of their team. I've heard them make the case that "it's too soon to do anything about the succession issue as we need the new staff to assimilate and the older staff needs time to build a more robust track record." I've witnessed CEOs who, when boards express skepticism about their chosen successors, create elaborate arguments for how "they might not be ready now, but they will be ready later." They insist that they don't want to fire a

C-suite member because he does a great job running his group even though he isn't ready to (and, importantly, may never be ready) to take over the CEO position and they also insist that if they were to bring in someone with better CEO potential, he or she probably wouldn't be as effective as the C-suite member in the short-term.

CEOs, however, need to realize that the board cannot let them be avoidant for long. In our current environment where boards must take continuity of leadership seriously, they are prioritizing CEO succession as a core part of their broader fiduciary responsibilities. They especially want CEOs to develop internal candidates because, if the board has to go outside to find a successor, it's often viewed as a failure of their governance.

My father had a phrase he used frequently, "Cooperate with the inevitable," and I would offer the same advice to CEOs. CEOs have to use the need for successors to their advantage—not see it as a threat to their continuity. Indeed, there are benefits to finding and developing the right succession candidate(s). Not only will these CEOs endear themselves to the board, but they'll model the type of mentorship behaviors that others in the organization will see and emulate.

An example of this challenge might be Denis Picard at Raytheon. Denis took over as CEO from Tom Phillips, who had been CEO/president since the 1970s. Picard had a unique, personally dominating style by which he guided Raytheon throughout the 1990s. Denis, though, was not one to mentor and train and develop others easily. He was demanding and hierarchal in his style, and while this produced solid results for shareholders, it did little to build a collaborative and mentorship enabled C-suite of executives ready to step up to the CEO role. When it came time for Denis to step aside, the board had to go outside, for the first time, to a competitor and appoint Daniel Burnham from another defense contractor to step up to be CEO. In so doing, the board effectively was admitting that they, and Denis, had failed to mentor the next generation of leadership for the company.

In addition, there's the legacy benefit. CEOs are judged not just by their performance during their tenure but by how their performance helps the company in the long term. Jack Welch of GE, for all his accomplishments, ended up being negatively affected by the mentorship and selection of successor when he named Jeff Immelt to follow him as CEO. Initially Welch received high praise for a very deliberate and highly transparent "run off" between four candidates to succeed him. When he and the board chose Jeff Immelt the choice received praise from many. Welch also ensured those he passed on would get great positions as CEOs of Boeing, Home Depot, and 3M. This process was widely hailed and provided a wonderful additional boost to Welch's distinguished leadership story. Yet, now several years later, the travail and problems associated with Immelt's tenure as GE's CEO have done little to further the Welch legacy and, in some circles, have tarnished what had been a shining legacy.

Therefore, CEOs should consider following the lead of companies like Emerson Electric, Abbott Labs, Danaher, and American Express which are widely recognized for ensuring senior executives are developed via corporate roles, in addition to their operational ones, so they can learn skills that go beyond their areas of expertise, developing the abilities needed for the top position.

Be aware, too, that a battle over succession between a board and the CEO can do great harm to the company culture. Many times, CEOs might favor a candidate they've been through the wars with and that they have come to trust. In doing so they might be easily blinded and not easily see the true readiness of the "loyal lieutenant" to step up to the more demanding CEO role. It is often very hard for CEOs to look dispassionately at their team and separate loyalty and followership from readiness to lead. CEOs need to be willing to ask themselves the tough questions about the true readiness for leadership the successor question requires. CEO's feelings and commitment to loyalty of another need to be set aside because boards are looking for CEOs to be dispassionate regarding their recommendations about successors. If boards suspect that a CEO is favoring his/her buddy, it can lead to serious conflicts that can have lasting effects.

For instance, consider the case of Sergei who was the head of a large, public company, had worked in the industry for a long period, and was widely recognized as a terrific CEO. He achieved much of his success because he had assembled and worked over time with a team of loyal executives who had traveled from one company to another with Sergei. When Sergei engineered a major transformative merger, he and his loyal team formed the core of the resulting industry-leading management team of the resulting larger, more prominent entity. Following the execution of this industry-shaping merger, the board appropriately asked for a successor plan for the CEO. Sergei was challenged to decide who from his team of loyal followers should be recommended as his successor. Eventually, Sergei felt obligated to choose the individual who had been most loyal and closest to him, despite the fact that his management style and leadership of others could be harsh and highly abrasive.

The board, however, had serious reservations about this recommendation since they felt the individual Sergei recommended was a great "number-two" leader but flawed in his ability to be a true CEO. Suddenly the board and the CEO were at odds on a fundamental question at a critical time in the new company's history.

The board suggested that another executive, who had joined the company two years previously as CFO after a stellar career elsewhere and who had distinguished himself in the merger, was a better successor. Initially, Sergei resisted the board's suggestion. In a series of meetings that grew heated, Sergei and board members debated the issue with increasing levels of recrimination and tension. Eventually, the board became adamant, and Sergei reluctantly deferred to the board's preference.

Sergei's chosen candidate was told he wasn't to be the successor and immediately resigned feeling chastened, having been all but guaranteed by Sergei that he would be the next CEO. He joined a competitor as the CEO heir apparent. With his departure and the ascension of the CFO to the COO role, the team that had once worked so well together was effectively disbanded. The C-suite team cohesiveness that was so central to Sergei's past successes had now ruptured. As well, Sergei's relationship with the board was negatively affected, and tension and animosity arose where none had existed before.

MENTORSHIP DO'S AND DON'TS

The importance of CEOs modeling mentorship behaviors is essential. Beyond just role modeling there are a number of other steps to encourage coaching, guidance, and sponsorship throughout the organization.

First, tailor mentorship to fit the mentee. Mentorship is a bespoke effort, never a one-size-fits-all. The mentorship role only works when it is custom-tailored to fit the needs of the individual and the context within which he or she operates. Some people may need more coaching than sponsorship. In other cases, mentors may need to focus their advice on specific situations and the lack of skills and experience that others have in dealing with these challenges. An individual may be struggling because he or she lacks a particular personality skill or is blind to the impact they are having on other members of the team. Another person may be a star but feels unappreciated by the organization.

The more mentorship addresses individual requirements, the more effective it will be. And the more effective it is, the more others in the organization will take note and adopt mentorship behaviors.

Second, keep in mind that formal mentorship programs are generally less effective than informal, organic ones. It is difficult to mandate mentorship. If you assign people to mentor others, the mentors can always go through the motions of mentorship without the desired commitment to the relationship. They may coach robotically, guide unenthusiastically, and sponsor rarely. Mentorship is highly personal, and people need to feel compelled and drawn to help those who are on their way up or struggling. Ideally, they see a connection between themselves and a mentee—they have the same interests, style, talents, attitudes. They want to help, and they are willing to put in the time and energy to do so.

Third, and this is a related point, don't expect HR to be singularly responsible for mentorship efforts. Yes, HR may run formal succession programs and progression reviews and incorporate the resulting data into a huge, color-coded database that puts people into various development slots. But slotting people into development groups is different than one-on-one mentoring. HR is a function and is by necessity focused more on the process and the scaling of such processes than on the actual quality and effectiveness of these very personal mentoring efforts.

Mentorship starts at the top, and the single best action that CEOs can take is to start choosing and mentoring their successors and make sure everyone in the organization is aware of their efforts in this regard.

7

Use Role Modeling as a Change Tool

Role-modeling behaviors is one of the most powerful tools CEOs possess but also one of the most underused. By articulating the ideas and modeling the desired behaviors that will further organizational objectives, CEOs can have a huge impact on culture, morale, and work practices.

Unfortunately, CEOs frequently undervalue the impact of their personal role-modeling activities such as how they allocate their time, what specific tasks they set as priorities, where they concentrate their focus, who they meet with and where they meet, and how they travel and who they travel with. These are but a few of the role-molding activities that are core for CEOs to model. CEOs are highly visible, and the way they conduct themselves in these dimensions of their everyday life provides a powerful weapon for trying to change a company's culture.

Besides undervaluing the impact of role modeling, CEOs are reluctant to see the signaling values of their own activities because they may not understand the power of their leadership role. In the required organizational behavior course that we teach to all our Harvard first year business students, we speak of "Leader as a beacon" to describe the importance of this leadership role. We use the analogy of the leader acting as a lighthouse and providing a beacon to illuminate the safe passage required to navigate difficult currents and dangerous shoals and reach an ultimate goal. The "Leader as a beacon" analogy emphasizes the CEO's role in spotlighting the behaviors, attitudes, and mindsets that should be emulated in order to pass through troubled waters.

Some CEOs also undervalue their own presence; they are modest, wish to appear to be egalitarian and demure and have others share the limelight. While some modesty and constrained sense of self is admirable, these CEOs must recognize that in most organizations, they are the true leaders, setting the tone for others to follow. While modesty and humility can be useful qualities for CEOs in many situations, they shouldn't blind CEOs to the need for and value of modeling the desired behaviors.

Another reason CEOs don't use role modeling sufficiently is because it's hard work. It's far easier to not worry every day how you'll be viewed by what you do, who you meet with, where you take your meetings, what you emphasize, how much time you spend on what topic, how pleasant or harsh your tone is, and so forth. It is exhausting, relentless, and just plain hard work. Of particular importance is the need for leaders to get out and be seen and engage others by walking around in headquarters or during tours of plants or sales offices. This exposes leaders to people they don't know and requires them to be inquisitive, personable, and caring. Some CEOs object to this level of engagement because some are surprisingly shy. Some don't like having to be constantly on display, others worry that they don't represent a productive use of their time, and some (in truth) might find these behaviors "beneath them"—they wish their executives and employees would just do as they say and not necessarily as they do.

AN ESSENTIAL CHANGE MANAGEMENT ASSET

The hard truth, though, is that CEOs often don't like to do the role modeling that is required to accelerate their change programs. As a consultant, I was always surprised by the comfort CEOs took in being in their own offices. It was the exception when I observed CEOs engaging working teams in their (the teams') working environments. For example, when doing major mergers and acquisitions and integration activities, CEOs were usually absent from the "war rooms" and rarely met informally with the integration teams. In most instances, they preferred formal reviews held in large conference rooms with many attendees. As a result, they received selective information, highly summarized and carefully framed in PowerPoint slides that masked the underlying facts of the true state of integration. CEOs willing to wander into the team rooms, sit down, and have an informal conversation with team leaders would have learned much more than what they gleaned from a traditional, formal communication method.

Similarly, it is more the exception than the rule that CEOs would go and visit major facilities without a carefully organized agenda with a preset series of meetings. The informal "dropping in" doesn't happen routinely. As a result, CEOs rarely just turn up at facilities. Meetings with suppliers and/or customers involve predetermined agendas, set expectations for who will be meeting with whom, and a sense of formality. As a result, the amount of learning and role modeling is quite limited.

I always admired an instructive story about the institutionalization of role-modeling behavior I heard about Walmart years ago. I was told that (for a time at least) Walmart store executives weren't allowed to submit an expense report for travel unless they had a written confirmation that they had stopped by a Walmart store and worked for a period of time with the store management team on the floor. This was a wonderful way to reinforce that leaders should practice role-modeling behaviors. While the threat of not reimbursing expenses may not be an ideal way to reinforce behaviors, it gets the message across.

Change programs are more likely to succeed when CEOs model newly desired behaviors. While employees usually understand the words behind the advocated changes, they often struggle to internalize what this means day-to-day and week-to-week. Besides not knowing how to translate lofty rhetoric into actions, many ask themselves, "Will I be alone if I undertake these changes?" There is safety in numbers; they want to be part of the change wave rather than the only ones out in front. CEOs need to go beyond outlining a change program. They must demonstrate elements of this change program by modifying their own behavior and with their senior team role-modeling actions that drive meaningful change.

While most of you are well aware of what role modeling means, you may not be aware of all the ways that CEOs can use this tool in the workplace. Therefore, we need to look at some specific applications.

FOUR WAYS TO MODEL THE RIGHT MESSAGE

Role modeling goes well beyond the efforts to consider how one is being viewed and ensuring one walks around a bit more than normal. It includes communication in all forms relative to beliefs, management processes, and change priorities that leaders try to encourage employees to embrace and act on. More specifically, CEOs possess a number of ways in which they can role model, including:

1. **Calendar management—how and where they spend their time.** CEOs' schedules are spotlighted, and their choices about how they spend their time—and the trade-offs inherent to these choices—send strong signals to their organizations. Their calendar management has to be consistent with their expectations for employee behaviors. How much time do you spend in the office versus traveling? Do you drop into team meetings

regularly or rarely? Are you spending the vast majority of your time on strategy and very little of your time on talent development?

For example, as I mentioned earlier, I spent time with Jack Welch when he lived in Boston, and at one of our regular lunches I asked him how much truth there was to the business press that said he spent upwards of 50 percent of his time on talent assessment reviews, staff training, and outreach on personal development. He said if anything the 50 percent *underrepresented* the amount of time he spent. He went on to say he did so to signal to everyone that this was a critical variable for GE's success and "if he could spend the time, so should they."

2. **Communication style and substance.** Beyond time and place, role modeling also means becoming more conscious about how you communicate. Consistent messaging underscores needed changes and incentivizes actions consistent with prioritized values and programs. For example, I work closely with the CEO of a pharmaceutical company that was embarked on a major turnaround who opened every board meeting with a review of the company's mission and what they'd done during the past period to deliver on that value. It was repetitive, but it drove home the message that their mission was valuable and they would live it consistently. When I asked him about it, he said it was his way of ensuring that he was truly role modeling the behavior the board expected him to deliver against the mission of the company.

I also often advise CEOs in the middle of a large merger or transaction to start every meeting, even one not dealing with the transaction, with a quick summary of why the transaction was being done. The subject of the meeting may have nothing to do with the actual transaction, but this represents an opportunity to remind everybody consistently why such a transaction was undertaken. Also since everyone wants to know details of such a major event (even though they might not be involved) and everyone talks about it, this is an effective reinforcement about the reason for the deal and a major communication device as well.

3. **Manner in which decisions are made.** CEOs should look at the wide range of choices facing them from a role-modeling perspective. What types of decision-making behaviors do they want their people to emulate? Do they want them to conduct extensive research before making choices? Do they want to always have and follow a formal decision-making process? Do they want to ensure that the decision is vetted by a diverse group? Senior staff and likely others who work for them will take their decision-making cues from CEOs. Since all decisions require trade-offs, it's important for a CEO to signal which trade-offs are important for the company to prioritize and the manner in which the CEO wants to see those trade-offs considered, with what attention to detail, with what risk profile, and so forth.

4. **Personal-professional balance.** CEOs also set the tone through their activities when it comes to finding the right work/life balance. Are they modeling a workaholic model? A traditional 9-to-5 one? If CEOs espouse the need for balance and time for personal reflection and family and then don't model this behavior, their message is watered down if not lost altogether.

MODELING THE RELATIONSHIP BETWEEN CUSTOMERS AND R&D

As I've suggested, role modeling can send a powerful message throughout an organization. One example is the way Jamie Houghton and Wendell Weeks—successive CEOs at glass giant Corning—led by example to pull the company out of its near-death experience in the early 2000s.

Houghton handed the reins to Weeks in 2005, and Weeks now runs a company that brings in more than $11 billion a year making glass for flat-screen TVs, optical fiber, ceramic substrates and particulate filters for emissions control in cars and trucks, glass packaging for the pharmaceutical industry, and the Corning® Gorilla® Glass that has become the gold standard for today's smartphones. The public company, based in Corning, New York, was run by the Houghton family for most of the company's nearly 170-year existence. Corning has always grounded itself in the values you might expect of a family-led company-town culture: Quality, Integrity, Performance, Leadership, Innovation, Independence, and The Individual.

During the dot-com boom of the late 1990s, Weeks ran the division that made optical fiber and fiber-optic equipment. As the emerging internet drove an explosion in demand for broadband digital communications, telecommunications companies such as AT&T and WorldCom aggressively built long-haul fiber-optic networks. The world's leading supplier of fiber for those networks was Corning. Amid the irrational exuberance of that era, the stock prices of dot-com and telecom-related companies rocketed to wild new heights.

At Corning during those years, Weeks' fiber division accounted for more than two-thirds of the company's profitability. By 2001, Corning's stock had raced to $113 a share, valuing the company at more than $115 billion.

Then it all collapsed. First the dot-com bubble burst in 2000. As internet companies closed or scaled back, broadband demand fell off. That exposed how much fiber networks had been overbuilt, and new construction all but stopped. Telecom stocks soon followed dot-coms into the hole. Corning's fell off a cliff. The stock dove to around $1 a share, valuing the company at $1.5 billion. The situation looked grave. As Weeks once said, "The institution was under attack."

Houghton, who had retired, returned as CEO to try to save Corning. A lot of CEOs might have instantly fired Weeks—the person who led the group that nearly crashed the company. Instead, in 2002 Houghton promoted Weeks to COO as a stepping stone to CEO. He told Weeks, "You helped screw this up; you help fix it." He also told Weeks that the company had been around for 150 years, and Weeks needed to come up with a plan that would help it thrive for another 150 years.

In role modeling, Houghton's actions sent a clear signal to the rest of the company. Promoting Weeks instead of bringing in an outsider showed a belief in Corning and its values. Houghton signaled a faith that the company could fix itself, and that others should have that faith and act accordingly. And for Weeks, the trust from Houghton gave him a determination to succeed—to not let Houghton or the company down.

Corning had become a dysfunctional collection of fiefdoms, with fiber as the wealthy favorite son and the rest feeling left out. Houghton and Weeks set out to change that and regain balance and teamwork, showing the way by spending time deep inside all of Corning's divisions, learning the details—in other words, role modeling how they wanted others to act.

Weeks followed up by reinforcing the message that Corning's culture and values were what made the company successful, not any individual product. By continuing to spend on R&D, Weeks showed that innovation would be a prized quality within the company. He didn't legislate this direction from on high. Instead, he got involved in finding new opportunities at the intersection of what customers wanted and what the company could innovate and deliver. He worked closely with innovation teams comprised of engineers, scientists, researchers, and marketers, and spent considerable effort to engage with customers.

In 2005, Weeks was named CEO. By then, Corning had 10 consecutive quarters of sales increases. It had developed the flat-screen display glass business, which now is the company's top profit generator. Weeks was intimately involved in the success of Gorilla Glass. It began with a meeting with Apple CEO Steve Jobs, who told Weeks about a new phone Apple was developing with a novel touch interface. Plastic covers that Apple had tried scratched too easily, and Jobs challenged Weeks to develop a thin, strong glass to create an all-glass touch screen on the front. Because Weeks had made the effort to know what was going on in Corning's labs, he knew of a type of glass first developed in the 1960s that could serve as an entry point for Apple's request, and he was able to tell Jobs he could make the glass for the phones on Apple's tight timetable. The story again sent the role-modeling message that success for Corning comes from close customer contact combined with Corning's innovative capabilities.

Weeks continued to exhibit this type of role-modeling in the pharmaceutical industry with the development of Valor® Glass. Weeks served as a member of Merck's board of directors from 2009 to 2020. In conversations with leading pharmaceutical companies, Weeks became aware that drug companies had long struggled with vaccine packaging. The conventional vials, made of a type of glass that had been around for a century, too often jammed or broke on pharmaceutical filling lines, cracked, or shed microscopic glass particles into the vaccine.

Weeks took the problem back to Corning's scientists, and they came up with a new type of glass far stronger than the old vials, with a low-friction exterior surface that allowed them to slide past each other on assembly lines, avoiding jams and breakage and increasing fill/finish production. As the world looks for a vaccine for COVID-19, Corning's Valor Glass vials are positioned to help accelerate vaccine production and availability.

As a symbol of Weeks' highly involved management style, his office desk—topped with pictures of family and friends—looks untouched and rarely used. One of the best ways to interact with Weeks is to take a walk with him around the various offices as he visits with teams.

As chairman and CEO, his role modeling shows everyone at Corning that success comes from engaging actively in the innovation process, working collaboratively across disciplines, listening for customer needs that Corning can solve—and, above all, believing in Corning's core values and people.

As a result, they follow suit. Consciously or not, employees observe their leaders and adopt their beliefs and modus operandi. It reminds me of how I learned to ski from my father. The first time on the slopes, he went in front of me and offered a single instruction: "Follow and do as I do." When I became better than him, I found others who had better skiing skills and followed them, mirroring their movements. The same mirroring process takes place in organizations, only it's the CEO who is out front.

THE MAGNIFICATION PRINCIPLE

CEOs have an impact above and beyond what they might expect their impact to be. Their actions and decisions are magnified in an era where their roles demand high levels of availability, visibility, and transparency. While CEOs have always occupied paramount roles in the lives of their organizations, many of them were often removed from the action: They spent a lot of time in their executive offices; they met with a single executive team; they often communicated with the company through memos. Today, CEOs are more actively involved with a diverse group of employees using all manner of communications approaches. They tweet and blog regularly, and they are expected to participate in a wide variety of headquarters, plant, community, and industry activities.

Their presence magnifies the effect of what they say and do. Roger Krone is a CEO who has used this presence to his organization's advantage. Roger, as you know from an earlier chapter, is the CEO of Leidos, a software services company that manages IT and other related systems for governmental groups in Washington, DC. The company has over 40,000 employees, and a key to their success is their ability to hire, retain, and develop individuals with unique skill sets required for the software and services they provide to a range of government clients. Roger underscores the importance of recruiting and maintaining this talent every Monday (when he is in Washington headquarters). He makes sure to stop in and attend one of the weekly orientation sessions for new employees. This benefits the new hires, but it also sends a loud and clear message about the importance of hiring and retaining talent. The new recruits hear this message and don't soon forget that the CEO met with them their first week on the job. It also gives Roger a way to communicate the company's mission. And finally, when Roger meets with his executive team and tells them that nothing is more important than the quality of people we hire, he can point to his Monday visits as a manifestation of this belief. Every executive in the room hears this and thinks, "He really means what he says … and maybe I could do more."

Sometimes, CEOs model behaviors that are bold and surprising, and this too can make a lasting impression. Earlier in Chapter 3, I described some of the constituency challenges Kodak CEO Jeff Clarke faced when he took over at perhaps the most difficult point in the company's history—traditional film and camera photography was rapidly becoming extinct. Filing for bankruptcy in 2012, the future looked bleak. They hired Jeff from the outside to become their new CEO, and one of his first acts was to reduce his considerable staff, since the move to digital resulted in huge shortfalls in Kodak revenue causing pronounced and permanent impacts. During his first week on the job, the board also asked him to decide whether Kodak should shut down the film business used by Hollywood studios in all their moviemaking.

It was a tough decision, but Jeff decided that shutting down this core business would be the worst possible thing to do, recognizing that the company needed to maintain its heritage if it was to survive.

Jeff went to Hollywood to talk with directors such as Steven Spielberg and Francis Ford Coppola, who were staunch advocates of film. After hearing their advocacy, Jeff told them that they needed to communicate their belief to the world, that film's quality is superior to digital. He stressed to these film directors that he couldn't keep Kodak's film division open for long unless they became vocal about their preference for film. They did as Jeff requested, and it helped Kodak survive.

While Kodak still has struggled and Jeff ultimately left as CEO, he worked to reemphasize the commitment to the customer he believed was going to be essential if Kodak was to survive. Through this decision process and the signals it sent, Jeff stepped out of the traditional CEO role and became an engaged and daring advocate. Few CEOs are willing to approach product influencers in order to save an iconic brand, convincing them to tell the world what they believe. Again, his actions had positive consequences internally as well as externally. He took a risk, role modeling the behavior he thought was needed to sustain Kodak.

BE CAREFUL ABOUT THE BEHAVIOR YOU MODEL

Role modeling is a tool that CEOs must also learn to use strategically. Role modeling is only as useful as the behavior being modeled. If you role model behavior that is old and antiquated or mirrors the operational approach that has gotten a company into trouble, then it obviously is counterproductive. Unfortunately, this effect isn't always obvious to CEOs who are caught up in their day-to-day responsibilities and may not be conscious of the effect their behavior is having.

I have mentioned Raytheon CEO Dennis Picard before. Now we will see the impact of his approach to management that was on display almost every week at Raytheon. Dennis was a superior project manager, possibly the very best in Raytheon's long history. As a defense contractor, the company must have managers who possess this capability since they live or die based on their ability to move efficiently from project to project. Dennis was brilliant at integrating engineering and marketing to meet project requirements with cutting-edge technology. Essentially, Dennis became Raytheon's supreme project leader for almost every major activity, investment, and program that Raytheon undertook. Most days you could go to Raytheon headquarters and find Dennis in the large conference room with project management teams lined up to see him in various offices. There could be as many as a half dozen project teams waiting to see him at any point during the day. While Dennis was able to add huge value and direct resources because of his ability to lead projects, his gatekeeping role inadvertently disempowered most of his people to take action without his review.

I experienced the bottlenecks that resulted from this process firsthand. When I had an appointment to see Dennis, I would ask his lead assistant how things were going, and invariably, she would tell me that they were running two to three hours behind. Efficiency suffered, and many would argue that it became part of the undoing of Raytheon and the reason Dennis' time as CEO didn't end as well as expected. The problem: Dennis was role modeling project management behavior, and while that had benefits for the organization, it also created significant problems.

Jim Kilts, Gillette's CEO, provides another example of a leader who did a lot of great things for an organization but also modeled behavior that had a counterproductive effect. Jim came to Gillette to help turn around this iconic Boston-based consumer products company. He was an outsider not only to the company but also to Boston. Jim was well known as a deal guy, having turned around Nabisco previously and selling it to RJR. Jim quickly assessed the need to pare the portfolio and improve operations and set about to do both. After enjoying initial success with these tactics, Jim encountered resistance to some of his ideas because of two concerns: how long Gillette would remain in Boston and whether Jim would sell the company the way he had Nabisco.

Jim did orchestrate a sale, and he certainly delivered value to shareholders. It's possible, however, that another, equally positive outcome might have occurred if resistance to Jim's moves hadn't surfaced. A number of Gillette's people noted that they never believed Jim was in it for the long term because he maintained his home in Scarsdale, New York, establishing temporary residence at a Boston luxury hotel. "How could I be committed to a massive change program on behalf of the future of the company if the CEO isn't willing to move to Boston and become a part of the community here?" was a typical refrain.

Jim modeled a short-term orientation to the company because he didn't establish a permanent residence in the Boston area. Especially for a CEO driving change, this behavior sends a strong message. CEOs intent on sustaining change and sustaining a culture have to model the behavior that makes these outcomes possible.

INSPIRATION AND INSTINCT

Here are two of my favorite stories about role modeling, one involving the head of my former organization and one a former NBA star and coach.

Marvin Bower of McKinsey was the founder of the modern management consulting industry and the firm's longtime managing partner. He was famous for espousing the importance of professional values. He wanted McKinsey to be run as a client-focused organization of professionals, more like a traditional counselor-based law firm than a traditional business. As a result, he talked constantly about the importance of maintaining high professional standards.

For years, Marvin would attend the introductory training program for all associates, who would spend half a day hearing from Marvin. How better to inculcate the mindset of professionalism than to have Marvin travel throughout the world to attend such sessions? Eventually the firm's scale and Marvin's age were such that he could no longer do this.

Nonetheless, Marvin found ways to continue modeling the need for professional values. McKinsey had a partners' meeting in Phoenix, Arizona, and one of the most powerful senior partners of the firm was presenting a plan for expansion into a new geography, which involved investments to secure new clients. The "business plan" that was being presented at the time included discussions of return on investment and suggestions around possible revenue expectations. Marvin was sitting in the back of the room and saw this for what it was—an encroachment on the professional values that he had so long espoused. In what has become a legendary moment within McKinsey, Marvin interrupted the presentation and in front of hundreds of partners engaged in a question-and-answer session with the senior partner as to how they could have a business plan that struck Marvin as challenging the firm's culture of professionalism. The senior partner was unable to satisfy Marvin, and only after the intervention of the managing director was Marvin willing to sit down. At that point everyone in the room gave Marvin a standing ovation, recognizing that he was modeling the behavior that we had all been trained to carry out.

Marvin has since passed away, but the videotape of this presentation and Marvin's intervention is shown to many of the new associates that join the firm. Even all these years later, the tape of Marvin's modeling behavior helps instill the professional values that are at the heart of the firm.

Maurice Cheeks and Marvin Bower have little in common in terms of their professions, but they share a role-modeling trait from which all CEOs might benefit.

If you're not familiar with Maurice Cheeks, he was a star basketball point guard for the NBA's Philadelphia 76ers as well other teams, and later he became the coach of the Portland Trailblazers. Right before a game between Maurice's Portland team and the Dallas Mavericks in 2003, the national anthem was sung by a 13-year-old girl. Or rather, she started to sing the anthem, but her nerves overtook her, and she forgot the words. Within seconds, Maurice moved with no hesitation to the girl's side, told her not to worry about it, and encouraged her to try again. Then he started singing the anthem and she joined in. Maurice had a terrible voice, but it didn't matter. Everyone in the entire stadium joined in, including all the players and Dallas coach Don Nelson (a notoriously crusty, no-nonsense man). It was a magical moment, and after the game Coach Nelson went into Portland's locker room and told Maurice that his gesture was one of the most impressive things he'd ever witnessed during his entire professional career.

Maurice responded to the potentially embarrassing situation instinctively and authentically. From that point on, Maurice probably never was doubted by his players when he talked about how they should support their teammates and sacrifice for the good of the whole team. He modeled that behavior in a way that made an indelible impression on anyone who saw it.

Like Marvin, Maurice acted in a way that was genuine and communicated desired organizational values. If more CEOs behaved this way, they could communicate their messages faster and with more effect than even the most eloquent mission statement ever could.

8

Use Psychic Rewards, Not Just Monetary Ones

One of the most powerful tools in a CEO's arsenal is financial incentives. The traditional corporate structure and hierarchal organization of most organizations ensures that we can incentivize the behavior of people by paying them to effect the change that we desire.

Most CEOs discover, however, that financial incentives are limited tools. In a moment, I'll discuss these limitations, but first, let's look at a counterpart to purely financial incentives: psychic rewards. These are emotion-based incentives that acknowledge people's performance and contributions, the way that individuals are made to feel valued and rewarded that plays to their psychic desire for recognition and reward. The sources of these rewards can include a public acknowledgment of a job well done, a private compliment, an award for superior productivity, or a plum team or committee assignment—the possibilities are many and varied.

Consider the value and power of such psychic rewards. UPS has a fleet of over 100,000 cars, vans, tractor trucks, and panel vans that are used to deliver over 20 million packages a year. UPS's problem is that these trucks are large, cumbersome to drive, and vulnerable to accidents, resulting in expensive repairs, insurance costs, and legal fees. If you are UPS, how do you motivate your drivers to drive more safely? UPS can and most likely does put in financial incentives for performance in route delivery. However, they also used psychic rewards in the form of a bomber jacket. A simple leather jacket with a fleece lining—what value could this hold for a driver? UPS awards this jacket to drivers who have a successful driving record without accidents for 25 years. 25 years! How could this be motivating? They receive not only the bomber jacket (which they can wear on their routes) but participate in a ceremony where their brown jerseys are retired and hung in the rafters of UPS buildings like the uniforms of legendary sports figures in stadiums. These drivers also receive special patches to wear on their uniform sleeves and privileged parking spots at their depots. As of 2013, about 1500 drivers, or 7 percent of all UPS drivers, had been inducted into this elite group. For the cost of a bomber jacket, UPS incentivizes their fleet of drivers and they create safer deliveries.

CEOs in all types of organizations can capitalize on the equivalent of bomber jacket incentives. Before focusing on how to use this psychic reward, let's return for a moment to traditional financial incentives.

SOLID BUT INFLEXIBLE

Financial incentives reflect the results orientation of the traditional corporation, the belief that tangible benefits should be given to productive employees. But in practice, hierarchical organizations require broad-base application of incentives and a need for equity in the manner in which compensation systems are applied. In many cases, collective bargaining or the need for alignment among similar groups of employees creates lock-step incentive structures. As a result, their incentive systems are not particularly agile. Tailoring financial incentives to fit individual objectives is difficult. Many agreements and other civil service–type requirements often mandate uniform implementation of financial compensation packages. To drive financial incentive-based change, specific criteria around objectives and measurement against those objectives must be in place.

In addition, the effectiveness (or what economists would term "utility") of cash incentives diminishes over time. While the need for financial compensation never disappears, the appeal and motivational value of every incremental payment diminishes after a minimum level is reached. Once employees achieve a certain salary or accumulate sufficient wealth, salary increases or bonuses no longer enjoy the same motivational power they once possessed. Over time, people are less likely to be motivated by the "appeal/greed" of compensation and more likely to value non-monetary rewards.

A relatively small number of elites, of course, do find monetary incentives motivating—accomplished athletes, film stars, major investors, and even CEOs. These few long for and demand financial remuneration and seemingly have an endless need to accumulate wealth. But for the majority of people it's not only the wealth per se that matters but what it measures over time. Those few in a position to make outlandish financial demands can and often do use their earning power as a measurement of their worth. Many see it as a benchmark to compare themselves with their peers.

For most employees that a CEO is trying to motivate, however, the financial incentives alone are of limited value if they don't possess a more meaningful component—a component capable of driving new mindsets and behaviors. Additionally, CEOs quickly discover that traditional financial incentive systems are incredible to implement, maintain, update, and keep consistent with ever-evolving regulatory and tax requirements. Financial incentives can be of limited value to employees; taxes, retirement, and non-cash adjustments, and deferred portions rewards and other factors also decrease their value. Determining the metrics to judge how well an individual or group has achieved their financial objectives is difficult, as is maintaining transparency and fairness.

When CEOs change incentives, they must wait for the delayed effect of changes to take hold—it can take months or even a year for the shift in objectives to play through. They also have to deal with the complexities of balancing components of these incentive schemes and hope that executives can see the link between desired behavior and their actual compensation package.

Given the inherent limitations of financial incentives, CEOs would be wise to broaden the type of incentives at their disposal.

INFORMAL AND FORMAL TYPES

The variety of psychic incentives available to CEOs varies considerably, but they can be grouped into two basic categories: formal and informal. The former involves actions that use existing structures and processes in corporate environments while the latter are more episodic and personality-based. Consider these examples:

Formal

Assignment to lead a committee

Leadership of a project-based activity

Representing a unit of the company or the company itself to an external audience

Selection for an external training program

An award/designation to recognize a quality assurance achievement

Opportunity to give a speech to an external or internal audience

Informal

Public praise

Invitation to address the board

Personal note or call from the CEO

Verbal approval in a meeting

The chance to sit with the CEO at a dinner table

Upgrading to first class rather than flying coach

Invitation to go to business school for training programs

These lists will vary considerably by organization, based on structures that are already in place (formal) and the imagination of the CEO (informal). As you look at both lists, however, you may wonder at the efficacy of these tactics, especially relative to traditional financial incentives. Therefore, let's examine some examples of psychic rewards and how and why they work.

When I was at McKinsey, I and my fellow partners were motivated by the desire to maintain the respect of our peers. We strove for client success and client impact, but ultimately the measure of our success was our ability to be respected by our fellow partners. This fundamental principle governed our entire review and compensation system. While a wide variety of qualitative factors determined our compensation, we were not measured on billings and utilization as much as we were on our ability to serve our clients with distinction and to be professionals respected by our colleagues.

While it may seem as if McKinsey, because of its culture and leadership position in the consulting world, is better suited for psychic rewards than most companies, any talent-based organization can capitalize on them. CEOs can use the psychological desire to be rewarded and recognized as performers in conjunction with a traditional pay-for-performance system. In fact, psychic rewards can function synergistically with traditional reward systems, each enhancing the other. When people feel they are receiving both fair compensation and fair recognition for their performance, they are likely to be doubly motivated to excel.

CEOs can also leverage psychic incentives to facilitate change efforts. Assignments to highly visible internal committees, selection for special projects, or noting an individual's contribution in front of colleagues can reinforce change program mindsets and behaviors. These rewards have the benefit of being individualized and easily implemented; they also have a major and immediate impact on how people are responding to efforts that require new ways of thinking and working.

Many different types of organizations have successfully used psychic rewards. Regions Bank in Alabama undertook a major cost reduction and efficiency improvement effort. At the end of it, the CEO of the bank sent personal thank-you notes (not emails, but handwritten notes) to all those who participated thanking them for their work—a simple gesture, but one that created great followership, a common understanding of what had been achieved, and the desire for others to be recognized as such for future programs.

Another CEO, Campbell Soup's Doug Conant, looked for a way to differentiate himself and drive change in a personalized and effective way when he took the job. As he said at the time, *"I was trained to find the busted number in a spreadsheet and identify things that are going wrong. Most cultures don't do a good job of celebrating contributions. So, I developed the practice of writing notes to our employees."* Conant would handwrite up to 20 notes daily celebrating employees' successes and contributions.

*"Over 10 years, **it amounted to more than 30,000 notes**, and we had only 20,000 employees."**

---

*Adapted from Duncan, Roger Dean. (2014). How Campbell's Soup's former CEO turned the company around. *Fast Company* (September 18).

CEOs can also use psychic rewards in more subtle ways. You may recall the Doug Parker example I cited earlier in which he became CEO of the merged American Airlines and US Airways. Plans were in place to roll out a new American Airlines logo and plane design when Parker took over, and the company had spent heavily on this effort—it represented a major departure from the company's iconic silver airplane design, recognized instantly throughout the world. Instead of moving forward with the livery project, though, Parker stated to all the senior staff involved with the merger that he was unsure if this redesign should move forward. He called a time out and requested that the entire employee group weigh in on this issue. By doing so, he was giving all employees—from both American and US Airways—a seat at the table. They ultimately approved going forward with the redesign, but the key was that Parker had rewarded people with recognition—he recognized their value to the merged company, and by soliciting their opinion, he communicated that they were all in it together.

WHY CEOS UNDERUTILIZE THIS VALUABLE TOOL

On first glance, an award or a congratulatory note may seem like small potatoes compared to more substantive rewards. Here's a negative proof: The real value of psychic rewards can be seen when they're taken away. Once again, recall Leidos' CEO Roger Krone. One of the early actions Roger thought to take was to phase out the use of service awards for tenure in the company. This was one of his early decisions when he became CEO, and his goal was to focus executives and employees on the new Leidos rather than the predecessor company. Executives and rank-and-file employees were vocal about their disappointment that this personalized, meaningful reward would be taken from them. Roger quickly recognized his mistake, reversed himself, and embraced the service awards that remain a centerpiece of Leidos' celebration of employee success. His intention was good—he wanted people to concentrate on Leidos' future rather than aspects of its past—but Roger, like many CEOs, underestimated the power of psychic rewards.

A second reason psychic rewards are also underutilized is because some of them require a significant time commitment on the part of the CEO. Recall Doug Conant at Campbell's writing all those personalized notes. Many CEOs would react like a kid whose parents demand he write personalized thank-you notes to everyone who gave him a birthday present. Not only would they have to invest time in the effort but it would also require them to depart from their CEO routines, doing things that they wouldn't normally do.

Third, CEOs may not use psychic rewards as much as they should because they can become fixated on pay-for-performance. After all, this is the basis for their own evaluation/compensation. Most organizations rely almost entirely on quantitative rather than qualitative measurement to assess performance, and they've relied on it for years. Quantitative measurements can be easily explained and justified. Qualitative ones, on the other hand, are less tangible and invite skepticism, especially from numbers-oriented people.

Fourth, CEOs have limits on what they can do in terms of compensation structures, and they may be leery of adding psychic rewards to their current system. They inherit existing pay structures that have been built up over the years, are widely recognized by employees, and usually have become imbedded in their companies' cultures. Auditors, compensation consultants, and benefit managers have all worked to approve the packages that are being offered. Regulators have approved the underlying formulas, and unions have agreed to contracts. As a result, most CEOs tread lightly when considering changing existing financial structures.

BUT COMPANIES CAN'T LIVE BY FINANCIAL INCENTIVES ALONE

This is the conundrum. While the four just-cited factors give CEOs pause about integrating psychic rewards into the mix, ignoring them renders existing structures less than optimal. Therefore, CEOs need to make changes in structures with the following realities in mind.

Pay for performance is and will remain the preferred incentive structure for almost every organization. Most companies lack the right elements for psychic rewards to be as pervasive as they are at McKinsey. In fact, McKinsey is an exception, able to capitalize on its collaborative, partnership-based culture and its profitability to include powerful emotional incentives. Most companies don't have these advantages, but that doesn't mean they should eschew psychic rewards.

Another reality: A commitment from leadership is necessary. Without a willingness to commit time and effort to implementing formal and informal psychic rewards, they won't happen. I accompanied the managing partner of McKinsey to meet with one of the leading money management firms in the world. The CEO of the organization was curious about McKinsey's skill at managing partners globally and how his company might develop this same ability. After the managing partner and I explained the peer evaluation process and the commitment to a committee-based review of individuals driven by the "respect of one's peers" notion, the CEO asked about the time commitment this process required. We explained it took up to 6–8 weeks of a professional's time to conduct these peer reviews. The CEO was aghast and, in language that I will clean up for the purposes of this book, said, "Why the hell would you ever do that? How could you possibly take your best performers and have them spend eight weeks just so that they could understand how they are respected by their peers? You guys are out of your minds." We were quickly excused from his office.

Yes, you must make a commitment, but realize that having an additional tool to drive desired change and motivate achievement of goals more than justifies this commitment. Remember, too, this important lesson my father taught me: Financial returns and incentives always have a depreciating and parabolic-like impact on one's life. Monetary compensation has a strong motivational benefit initially. Above some minimum threshold, however, the incremental value of continued financial incentives declines. Over time, the value of monetary rewards alone diminishes. However, the value of psychic rewards is not limited in this way. People are driven to get rewards that differentiate them from others or make them feel good about what they have accomplished, regardless of their financial compensation. Receiving kudos from a leader never gets old. On top of that, formal and informal incentives are numerous and varied, keeping these incentives fresh.

Be aware, too, that if you want to change the mindsets of senior leaders, psychic rewards are far more effective than monetary ones. The latter are usually designed to catalyze behavioral changes (outputs), but when you need leaders to shift their perspective or develop a new theory of the case, then psychic incentives are necessary. They not only help change mindsets, but they also produce sustained behavioral change as well.

Roger Bannister's story demonstrates the value of mindset change. As an English university student, he broke the four-minute mile mark in 1954, and Bannister has been celebrated over the years for this breakthrough accomplishment. For many years before this, no one had been able to run a mile in under four minutes, and many assumed that it was an unbreakable mark until Bannister's feat. What many people don't remember, however, is that just 45 days later, Australian runner John Landy also ran a sub-four-minute mile, setting a new record and beating Bannister's. Less than one year later, three other runners accomplished the task of running sub-four-minute miles.

What changed? How could this seemingly unbreakable mark stand for decades and then be broken by five runners within one year?

It wasn't a new running technique or better training or nutritional supplements. It was a changed mindset. Bannister showed that the four-minute mile mark was not unassailable. Having achieved that objective, it was easier for others to do the same, if not better. Today over 1400 male runners have achieved a sub-four-minute mile.

CEOs should be aware of the value of a change in mindset. They need leaders to transition from a belief in hierarchy to a belief in teams, from a following-orders mentality to one that embraces disruption. You can't "pay" for this shift, just as it wouldn't work with Bannister and the other runners as sole motivation to break the four-minute barrier. In that competitive environment, their sense of self and sense of athletic achievement was tied to reaching and bettering a milestone.

9

Get on Board with Your Board

Historically, CEOs have always had a complex relationship with their boards of directors. Ultimately, a CEO's board is their "boss" and can (and does) hire and fire them. Boards are also the fiduciary with legal responsibility to represent the shareholders' best interest, putting them in a potentially contentious relationship with the CEO. Yet it is the CEO who is running the company and making the critical decisions essential to maintaining the performance and health of the business. The CEO works tirelessly to make the daily trade-offs essential to the success of an enterprise and worries every day about the impossibly wide number of issues that have to be considered in running a business. Yet it is the board that flies in for quarterly meetings lasting one or two days that assesses, questions, judges, and critiques much of what the CEO does. Boards are the final arbiter of CEO performance even though members have never put in the many hours of work or accumulated the depth of knowledge that CEOs have. This isn't a knock against boards; it's just an acknowledgment of a little-discussed reality that makes the CEO/board relationship a challenging one.

No CEO is going to say that they don't value their board or that they're not a helpful partner in running and growing the enterprise. So don't look for a CEO to broadcast this hidden truth: The CEO's relationship with their board is almost always challenging, at times taxing, often contentious, and always requires constant attention. To manage this complex relationship effectively, CEOs take different approaches and some choose to not always be fully forthcoming with their boards about all the many details of their company operations or not allow interactions with the management team. Indeed, some treat their boards as necessary fiduciary checkpoints mandated by corporate governance policies rather than as fully valued partners.

We live and work in complex, volatile, challenging times. No CEO is an island, entire of him- or herself, and the trade-offs and critical decisions leaders need to make are now larger, come more frequently, and are more demanding that any time in the past. Leaders need all the help they can get, and boards are a built-in if underused resource. Boards possess incredibly valuable wisdom—they are a source of unbiased advice and are the ideal group to bounce ideas off—and it's up to CEOs to be far more proactive in tapping it than they ordinarily are.

Equally challenging, for both boards and CEOs, is that this is also an era of increased accountability. Boards are under pressure to hold CEOs accountable, and they need to be far less forgiving than in the past as they have to ensure they satisfy the demands of shareholders, stakeholders, and communities. This puts further pressure on the relationship.

The hidden truth is that the traditional, strained, and for the most part "keep separate" CEO-board relationship is becoming an anachronism, and CEOs need to take the lead in embracing a more modern way to manage their boards. The closer we look at the current environment, the more compelling the case for CEOs to forge new and improved relationships with boards.

TIMELY FACTORS

As a consultant, I've had a bird's eye view of how the relationship has evolved. One catalyst for this needed evolution has been the increase in challenging mergers, acquisitions, and other transactions, requiring CEOs and boards to be upfront with each other about the problematic issues involved.

I was a part of a team that was retained to aid a major food company when they bought a competitor. As part of my team's responsibilities, we prepared regular board reports—updates about the pace and integration of this acquisition. After submitting drafts that included details on both the transaction's positives and the challenges, we saw from their final edits that the management team chose not to share the wide variety of various integration challenges that accompany any large transaction of that scale. Management were more comfortable with updates on the process rather than on our conclusions about the increasingly challenging and slowed pace of the integration. After management's edits, the board received information such as how the new organization would look, when and how many people would be moving from one headquarter city to another, how many facilities were now having to be consolidated, and updates on combined finances and needed IT system integration timing. However, the board didn't have access to the doubts and uncertainties that many of their leaders were harboring toward the acquisition. Fundamental issues around the quality of the acquired customer franchises and worries about the management team and their operating culture were not being shared. With more transparency and a different historical relationship between the board and the management team, these doubts and uncertainties might have been communicated; and they may have prompted the board to ask pointed questions and provide greater guidance about the acquisition. The fault lay not only with the senior management; the board also didn't do its job. I recall attending a few of the meetings during these integration updates and being amazed how uninquisitive the board was and how few detailed questions they asked of management about such a major acquisition.

I played a similar role for a beverage company when they were vertically integrating their bottling/distribution network into the company and for a pharmaceutical business after they had bought a competitor. Both acquisitions had large cultural conflicts because the acquired entities were so operationally different than the existing companies. You would have thought the boards would spend considerable time on these challenges and seek to understand how to mitigate these differences and smooth the integration of multi-billion dollar businesses. Here again, the focus was more on the process of integration and less on the huge cultural challenges. Once again, the boards had some clear notion of these challenges but rarely asked for how these organizations were bridging the cultural divide.

This isn't unusual, in part because corporate leaders can be guilty of being relentlessly and sometimes dangerously positive. A February 21, 2018, a *Wall Street Journal* article examined General Electric's "success theater" and a culture that turned a deaf ear to negative news. As a result, their board may not have transparency into just how serious the problems facing GE Power were until months after CEO Jeff Immelt had departed.

Recently, I had occasion (as part of a board role) to interview a major C-suite player from the power generation business that was a major causal factor for GE's poor returns and Immelt's retirement. Key to this failure was the ill-advised $11 billion purchase of French-based Alstom at what turned out to be the top of the market. I asked the executive why the deal had occurred after she had observed (defensively) that she and many on the executive team had huge doubts about the acquisition. She said that the CEO's desire for the deal and the benefit of scale that it would deliver was of critical strategic importance and it would have likely cost anyone on the senior team their credibility and likely their jobs if they had objected. Even more disturbing, this executive said that in

her view, the board wasn't given enough background to fully
assess where in the market cycle the business was and seemed
to be uninterested in challenging the CEO's underlying deal
assumptions. Both the CEO and the board failed in their
managerial roles. The CEO was fired, the board was rightfully
criticized for their lack of oversight, and many others were
replaced by the new board chairman and eventual CEO of
GE, Larry Culp. These examples remind us why CEOs must
embrace and use their boards and why boards have to work
harder to be more inquisitive.

The challenge of managing M&A isn't the only reason for
using boards more effectively. Today, at a time when organizations are not only merging and acquiring but attempting
to blend teams, divisions, and other groups to foster greater
diversity and ensure seamless global operations that meet
stakeholder as well as shareholder needs, leaders require the
wisdom of their boards to facilitate integration.

The complexity of issues challenging organizations in
recent years demands all hands on deck, and yet CEOs fail to
recognize that they're working with less than a full crew. At
the time of this writing, the world is gripped in the throes of a
pandemic that has effectively shut down commerce around the
world. The global economy and the social/political challenges
that businesses have to deal with are enormous, and making
matters worse, no historical precedent exists on which they
can draw. Organizations are facing huge unknowns, and
CEOs need the wisdom of the many to deal with the crisis.
During this time, boards are in frequent emergency meetings,
being updated about the scale and impact of the virus and
hearing plans for mitigation within organizations. It will be
fascinating to see how many CEOs and their boards work
together to jointly face the unknown challenges ahead.

A broader caution has emerged from the current crisis.
A CEO was relating to me that he was having to respond to the
US government demands for them to shift production to produce needed health care test equipment in short supply. He
was relating how the government was naïve in their demands

because the company was only an assembler of the components that made up the needed equipment; Asian export controls and lack of source materials had made it impossible to ramp up product production. I asked how he was dealing with this and what his board believed should be done. The CEO said he had spent the last three weeks dealing with this issue and that his board "doesn't know and doesn't really care as they rely on me to come up with the answers. I'll tell them how we resolved the issue when we figure out what to do." This is a time when CEOs need boards' ideas and feedback. That this CEO chose not to tap into a valuable resource during a crisis—whether because the board really was indifferent or this was the CEO's perception—was a lost opportunity. It made one wonder how many other CEOs were failing to capitalize on their boards during crises.

Beyond the Coronavirus crisis, consider just some of the most recent issues that managements and boards have to deal with: employee discrimination lawsuits, team-based restructuring, responses to ramped-up global competition, the need for digital transformation, the pursuit of disruptive innovation, and rise of activism in all forms. The Me-Too movement, climate change, and income disparity challenges all create thorny issues for senior leadership and boards. Failing to use a valuable resource to meet these challenges isn't acceptable. Consider the recent failures of Uber, Volkswagen, WeWork, Pacific Gas and Electric, and Boeing's boards and the concomitant failure of many CEOs, and it's obvious that CEOs and boards need to work more closely together.

Collaboration between CEOs and boards has to improve if for no other reason than it buys time for CEOs to effect needed changes. CEO tenure is becoming increasingly short. According to an article in the *National Association of Corporate Directors* (October 5, 2019) headlined "CEO Departures Hit Record High," 1009 CEOs resigned in the first nine months of 2019. As the article points out, some of these CEOs were "pressured to resign"; others, like WeWork co-founder and

CEO Adam Neumann, were fired by their boards. CEOs are more vulnerable than ever before, and the pressure to deliver results starts sooner rather than later. It's in their best interest as well as the best interest of their companies to establish a more open, more engaged relationship with their boards.

Boards, too, have compelling reasons to seek greater involvement in the critical issues facing their companies. The NACD Blue Ribbon Commission report *Fit for the Future: A New Imperative in Board Leadership* stated that "Boards must engage more proactively, deeply, and frequently on entirely new and fast-changing drivers of strategy and risk, [which will entail] being more actively engaged in challenging management's thinking, and when appropriate, acting as a thought partner with management in order to effectively respond to new strategic challenges."

PROACTIVE, NOT REACTIVE

Engaged CEO-board relationships don't just happen. Someone has to manage the relationship, and the best CEOs are sufficiently confident and forward-thinking to do so. Instead of passively accepting the relationship as it's always been, they see the value of making an effort to change it for the better.

This proactive attitude is especially relevant for CEOs who inherit their boards (as compared to choosing their board after a merger or some other type of transaction). They must get to know board members—from their expectations to their operational preferences. They also must figure out who on the board wields the most influence and generates followership. Admittedly, this takes time and effort, and many CEOs discover they have little to spare given all their other operational and strategic priorities. Yet it's critical for leaders to identify, understand, and reach out to the lead director and other highly influential board members frequently and avail themselves of this significant resource.

This doesn't mean just having a sidebar with a given individual at a regularly scheduled board meeting. True connection requires a greater effort. Specifically, here are three recommended actions:

1. **Engage board members in a social setting that isn't the boardroom.** If board members live in another city, fly there to meet with them. CEOs need to be willing to extend themselves. When the CEO summons others, it puts them in a subservient position. By meeting board members on their home turf, it sets the stage for an honest, productive, relational conversation.

2. **Show humility balanced with confidence.** Too often, leaders feel compelled to express a strong viewpoint, especially when they are beginning their CEO tenure. Too often, new leaders are overly worried about appearing indecisive or weak, especially in front of board members. It's good to be confident, but this should be balanced with a willingness to listen. For instance, ask board members to connect you to someone else. Request that they allow you to tap into their networks for a particular type of expertise. This is a fabulous ask on which CEOs often fail to capitalize. It acknowledges to board members that you don't know everything and that you value what and who they know.

3. **Consider allowing the board to work with your team.** Admittedly, this is a controversial recommendation for some companies that believe the line separating the board and senior management should be strictly observed. Still, it is a tool that can help CEOs forge stronger connections with their boards and leverage their subject matter expertise. In the past, most CEOs kept boards away from their teams. Allowing board members to get to know/work with the senior team not only benefits the senior team, but it informs the board as to the quality of that team and the challenges this team presents for the CEO. It draws the board and the CEO

closer as they share insights and development priorities with senior staff. Finally, it deepens and enhances the richness of the relationship between the board and the CEO.

A REFLEXIVE RELUCTANCE

You would think that given the enormous challenges facing leaders today, they would embrace the opportunity to form real partnerships with their boards. As strong and confident as CEOs appear, many are insecure and unwilling to be vulnerable. They feel if they reach out to their boards for active help, they'll be viewed as weak or indecisive. As a result, they limit the board's unobstructed view of the corporation's strategy, operations, staffing, and results.

Despite the shifting definition of leadership—the move toward a more vulnerable, transparent, and egalitarian leader—many CEOs still see themselves as captain of the ship. They don't welcome having their decisions questioned and the rationale needing to be explained to others. They like being at the helm and guiding the company based on innate knowledge rather than having to actively consult on change of directions. While they may recognize a new, enlightened attitude—they always talk about how great their boards are—their actions often fly in the face of what they say. Many view boards as potentially intrusive, as people they "have to" deal with rather than "seek to" deal and work with.

As a result, CEOs often prefer show-and-tell relationships with their boards: They show them the numbers, tell them what they're going to do, and hope to achieve easy consensus and approvals in response. In the short run, maybe this is easier. But it's not better. Numerous studies reveal that CEOs who connect deeply and continuously with their boards—who share their doubts and aspirations as well as the results—are not only personally more successful, but their company performance improves.

THE RESET OPPORTUNITY

As a new CEO, you're either replacing someone or taking over after a merger or acquisition. In both cases, you have an opportunity to reset your board. You can change how you deal with them as well as seek to change who is on your board. While you can't take the latter action immediately, you have a window in which to make decisions about board members. Practically and from a regulatory standpoint, you can't easily replace large numbers of board members. However, sometimes just changing one or two critical members can make all the difference. It should come as no surprise that Uber swapped out several board members when its new CEO took over from the founder. The SEC demanded that Tesla change its board after Elon Musk was reprimanded for acting in controversial ways. The PG&E board was restructured in response to the failure of the company after the California wild fires debacles. WeWork recast its board after its failed IPO and its founder was ousted.

It's much easier to make such changes as part of a merger or acquisition, since you negotiate how many board seats you're going to retain from the merged/acquired company board.

Resets aren't just occasions for bringing in new board members but for reconfiguring their working relationship with the board. Doug Parker at American Airlines established an open and transparent relationship with his board that was far different from the one his predecessor had. Bob Comport at Keurig Green Mountain built a very open and engaged relationship with his board following the company's purchase of Dr Pepper.

Don't let the reset period and the opportunity it represents pass you by.

When I was at McKinsey, the managing partner would often accompany me on visits to new clients, and he would meet with new CEOs and always inquire, "Tell me about your board." He was reminding CEOs of the board's importance and the need to formulate a productive relationship with them. He was also assessing how the client CEO thought of themselves, how confident they were in their management style, and their openness to receiving counsel and adapting their views. Attitudes toward and actions related to boards provide valuable insights about CEOs. Are they willing to seize the reset moment and make what can be difficult changes to a board that supports their management philosophy and strategy?

Here's another motivating factor for taking advantage of reset opportunities: Some board members aren't fully engaged in carrying out their mandates.

The hidden truth is that just because a board member has had an illustrious career filled with accomplishments doesn't mean that they will be as dedicated to being effective and active in their board position. Years ago, I was talking to a very senior Boston-based CEO who was on the board of one of this country's largest, most prestigious commercial banks. This bank had been highly acquisitive, having bought several major banks and other financial institutions in the last 12–18 months. When I remarked to this board member that he must be very busy with board-related responsibilities (given all these acquisitions), he said, "Not really. I get a board book on Friday, I am flown to [the headquarters city] on Monday, and I'm asked to vote to approve the acquisitions on Tuesday." I asked how could he provide informed advice and counsel given the compressed time frame, and he explained that the CEO really didn't seek advice and counsel. Why, I asked, was he staying on the board if he was just rubber-stamping the CEO's decisions? He said, "It's a prominent board, and I'm pleased to have been asked."

Be wary of boards that include people who are happy to be asked and to show up but whose advice and counsel are not the result of solid homework and an active commitment to the institution and its success. Sense if they're going through the motions; if and when you have an opportunity to replace them, you should.

Similarly, be aware that some board members may not only be serving for the prestige but also for the money. This may come as a surprise, since the assumption is that board members have had highly successful careers and have been well-compensated and serve more for the ability to contribute than for the remuneration. Certainly this assumption is true for most of the boards but not all. Board members may be in situations where their board salaries plus equity awards represent significant compensation.

There's nothing wrong with being paid for your expertise, but when financial gain is a main motivation to serve on a board, it can create problems. I know of a prestigious consumer-oriented company that was in deal discussions to complete a sizable transaction. I had been asked to assess how to structure the integration, as the CEO had assumed the deal was a fait accompli. Then I received a call from the CEO informing me the board had turned down further consideration of the deal. The problem: Three of the board members thought they would lose their positions and were objecting that the CEO hadn't negotiated hard enough in the initial stages to ensure the continuation of the acquiring board. When I probed further, the CEO admitted several of the board members likely "needed the compensation."

CHOOSING BOARD CHALLENGERS

Obviously, you don't want to choose mean-spirited board members who are focused on themselves and do not work well with others. Nor do you want to select veteran executives who provide prominence to the board but who no longer want to make the necessary commitment of time and energy.

When you have the opportunity to select board members, do so as a result of a consciously, purposeful search rather than acting reflexively and too quickly. Too often, CEOs can opt for "safe" standard types of board members rather than taking the risk to go outside the box and select candidates that can bring a range of perspectives. These board candidates include those who are senior, experienced, curious, and willing to challenge CEOs with their ideas and recommendations. Understandably, perhaps, leaders are wary of having these opinionated people "looking over their shoulder." This is flawed logic. Leaders should be warier of passive boards rather than individuals who provide wise, if occasionally challenging, counsel.

RESTRUCTURING BOARD INTERACTIONS

It's not just who's on the board but how they work together that counts. While organizations often have protocols in place to govern these interactions—designated meeting times, places, and procedures—CEOs can and should revisit these protocols and change them with an eye toward increased board effectiveness. Doing so may seem heretical—but it can pay big dividends.

Here are some of the changes that have been suggested to me as ways to improve and reset the board dynamic.

- **Be mindful of your lead director relationships.** Most CEOs realize that creating a strong relationship with the lead director is essential, but thinking of this director as the "driver" can be a mistake. The loudest voice in the room may not be the most effective voice. CEOs need lead directors who can "orchestrate" discussions and decisions, not ones who speak frequently and fervently. More important is a lead director who can orchestrate a synergistic relationship between the CEO and the board. This orchestrator can also keep the CEO informed about who the loudest, most challenging voices on the board are. When CEOs aren't present, these board members are most likely to share their concerns and expectations. An orchestrating lead director can make sure the CEO is aware of these views and will address them sooner rather than later, preventing them from simmering for months and then boiling over. Also, bringing the board member with the most powerful voice "inside the tent" in many cases is better for the board dynamic than having them on the outside always questioning and appearing to be challenging the view of management.

- **Provide boards with greater insights and less data.** Some CEOs respond to the need for transparency by over-whelming their boards with data. I have seen pre-meeting books that contain upwards of 500 pages of material. Ironically, this "generous" sharing of data obscures what's important—so much data exists that it's difficult for board members to separate the wheat from the chaff. The result: Board meetings turn into Q&As around specific pieces of data, not broad thematic discussions.

  A much more productive focus would be to create a holistic sense of where the business is today and where it needs to go. This can be done through greater staff analysis and CEO-summarized conclusions. Yes, this means your staff must spend more time on this task, and it may produce questions and even criticism of senior management strategies. But this is a far better outcome for both CEOs and their organizations than the data games played in board meetings that bog members down in the weeds of facts and figures.

- **Loosen up the overly formal meeting schedule and structure.** It's easy to get locked into the traditional board meeting format. Typically, board meetings are two-day events with short committee meetings during the first day followed by a dinner and then a formal board meeting on the second day. PowerPoint presentations that repeat much of data handed out before the meetings dominate the sessions. As I noted earlier, these presentations can devolve into "show-and-tell" events where members are encouraged to listen and comment lightly rather than ask tough questions and probe deeply. The full board meeting on the second day tends to repeat much of what was discussed during committee meetings, with the addition of procedural motions (required by regulatory statute) and the CEO's brief opening and closing perspectives.

If this pattern is familiar, you need to ask yourself what you might do to vary the pattern so as to create richer, more analytical discussions—discussions that yield productive ideas and advice.

Leaders could consider less formal, more boots-on-the-ground options to traditional meetings. Too often, boards meet in large boardrooms with lots of support staff, isolated from the actual operations of the company. A better option to consider is having board meetings in major operations centers, distribution facilities, and in nontraditional markets, so that members can observe the work of the corporation and employees. I learned the value of this lesson early on when my father, who was on the Texas Instruments board, would return from his board meetings talking about how much he had learned from off-site travels—to manufacturing facilities, overseas markets, and visits with customers and end-users of their products. It was hard, time-consuming work but fulfilling for him as a board member and for the management team that he worked with.

Getting out of the big boardroom is healthy for everyone. Schedule field trips, hold meetings in local markets, spend time with employees other than the senior executives as well as customers and other stakeholders. As leaders, CEOs should be sufficiently confident to break with the past and establish new, more productive traditions.

I sit on the board of the family-operated JM Huber, and board members spend time with our shareholders—the Huber family. Every year we attend their family gathering and we talk with them throughout the year about the challenges and the results of the business. We also spend time with them as individuals getting to know them and understanding their perspectives and interests. We travel to manufacturing sites; we meet with frontline management of those sites and in those markets so we can better understand the businesses. We tour manufacturing facilities and spend time and Q&A with the line management rather than just hearing from a senior executive.

Yes, it's a family company, and this meeting dynamic is entirely different for public companies with shareholders and analysts as part of the mix. At the same time, the private company experience is one from which public companies can try and emulate and learn from. It's not heresy to break with CEO-board traditions: It may be disruptive, but that's the point.

WILL BOARD MEMBERS RESIST?

Some board members might not appreciate deviations from the traditional norms they have used in the past. Yet the resistance can be an indicator of where the board is with regard to its own development. Resistance might mean the board is too stuck in the past and unwilling to adapt to the needs of the present and future—useful knowledge for CEOs. Also, much of the unwillingness to change rests with CEOs. Their openness to experimentation and willingness to shake things up, especially when first appointed to the CEO job, has a lot to do with why some new measures such as the ones discussed here aren't implemented. They also may be unwilling to invest the time, effort, or, in some instances, the money, to make these changes happen.

No doubt, some board members relish the pampering, prestige, and known routines of traditional board meetings. The carefully planned logistics, the ever helpful staff, and the lovely dinners all are nice perks.

If you're a CEO, however, you need to ask yourself: How much is the formality and privilege of your board meetings contributing to the business? What expense in terms of time, effort, planning, and preparatory expense is incurred? What would you gain if you experimented with changing some of the traditional elements?

Here's another surprising truth: Good board members don't want or need a lot of these luxuries. What they do want and need is to feel like their opinions are valued, that they're working in concert with the CEO and the corporation to ensure balanced operations, and able to be proud of the corporate environment and results to which they're contributing. CEOs must make the effort to ensure that their board members are focused on engaging in the actual work of the corporation.

10

Do Good While Doing Well

Today's leaders must find a way to manage this frustrating paradox. The complexity of the corporate, social, and political environments today requires that CEOs must do more than satisfy the commercial needs of their organizations. They must also role model desired behaviors and meet societal demands for good corporate citizenship while delivering financial and operational results. It is no longer acceptable to satisfy shareholders without also finding the time and marshaling the resources to meet the needs of various stakeholder groups—environmentalists, employees, retirees, community advocates, state regulators, and many others. Ignorance of these EHS issues (environment, health, safety) can often put organizations into potentially explosive situations that play out negatively in the public domain.

In recent years, boards and CEOs have become increasingly attentive to the complaints and concerns of an ever increasing array of stakeholders. Social media and community activism have awoken consciousness around environmental concerns, appropriately invited scrutiny around sourcing from developing markets, and called attention to the treatment of disadvantaged populations, income inequality, and "Me-Too" issues, as well as the racial justice movement issues. As a result, leadership attention has by necessity had to balance stakeholder as well as shareholder requirements. CEOs are under tremendous pressure to respond, and expected to be public role models showcasing their organization's informed, caring, and attentive attitudes to these stakeholder issues.

The hidden truth is that leaders don't realize how much pressure they'll feel to satisfy stakeholders and how it may compromise their ability to do so. Most CEOs understand that market demands are such that shareholders must remain their primary priority, but they also realize that they must now balance the sometimes conflicting and always important concerns of stakeholders. This understanding, however, can be threatened by the volume and omnipresence of these demands. Some leaders may be tempted to lean too far in the direction of stakeholders at the expense of shareholders—a potentially big mistake because of the inherent need to meet operational and financial expectations of boards and investors. Or they may ignore stakeholders and devote all their attention to shareholders—also a mistake since society at large, community interests, and boards demand they do both. Failing to make these trade-offs invites the scrutiny of many external advocacy groups and the media, who are poised to investigate and call out behavior they feel is egregiously offensive to stakeholders.

And therein lies the paradox: How can CEOs find the right balance between these two competing demands, given limits of time and resources?

SAYING ONE THING, DOING ANOTHER

Today's leaders care deeply about income inequality; they are sensitive to climate change issues; they strive to ensure safe, diverse, and caring work environments. No leader today is going to say (or believe), "Frankly, I am going to ignore stakeholder issues so as to make the analyst community and Wall Street happy with terrific results." Every day, it seems, our society ratchets up demands for greater organizational attention to hot-button issues. Indeed, the Business Roundtable, an association composed of CEOs, produced a statement in 2019 that called for a greater organizational focus on community, environment, and societal concerns, adding that although shareholders are important, they are only one component of a broader perspective.

Board members at several companies have told me that although their CEOs signed this Business Roundtable statement, they were really communicating the following: Being a signatory was "the appropriate thing to do" but they assured their boards that "we run our business this way (with stakeholders in mind), so we'll still deliver for our shareholders." In essence, these CEOs were in some ways placating their boards, communicating that there was no substitute for shareholder satisfaction, and that "equal" trade-offs between shareholder and stakeholder requirements weren't always possible if they were to achieve desired shareholder outcomes. Board members have told me many stories (or I have observed) CEOs who would begin board meetings by focusing on all the good they and their senior team had done—from charity events to environmental cleanups to diversity hiring and training. While all the board members were genuinely impressed by the CEOs' commitments to make the world a better place, most admitted to me they were still thinking, "But what are you doing about ensuring we meet guidance to the street for the coming quarter?"

It's a supremely tricky balance. Leaders shouldn't underestimate the forces driving their organizations to engage with stakeholders. Blackrock is a huge asset management firm whose influence is tied to their minority holdings in huge numbers of companies. Larry Fink, the head of Blackrock, wrote a letter to CEOs of companies represented by their funds that created a stir in 2018. Fink essentially told them that they could no longer just worry about their shareholders;

they had to worry about stakeholders in all their communities. This was followed by similar statements from investment management companies Vanguard and State Street. Blackrock and Fink brought even more focus to stakeholder concerns by adding climate change as a criterion for their review. Many CEOs have responded that it's great that Blackrock has taken this position, but they privately ask why it is that they are still faced with questions from their analysts (including those from the organizations writing these letters), and others like them, about how they are also going to deliver on their quarterly commitments. As one CEO lamented to me, "It's the CEOs who have to deliver, not Blackrock."

This paradox isn't just frustrating for CEOs; it's personally threatening to the CEOs' tenure. More CEOs were fired in 2018 than in any previous year. Their jobs are on the line, and if they get the balance wrong—if they spend too much time on programs they're passionate about such as climate effects or income disparity or workplace diversity and not enough time building their global business—then they're gone.

The academic world, too, contributes to this emphasis on a new approach to managing the broadening group of stakeholders. The widely renowned and highly talented Johb and Natty McArthur University Professor, Rebecca Henderson, has been at the forefront of Harvard Business School's increasing efforts to bring greater visibility to these trade-offs. Rebecca has begun offering a course titled, "Reimagining Capitalism," which raises this issue among students, and has now authored a new book entitled *Reimagining Capitalism in a World on Fire*, which informs this debate surrounding corporate responsibility to a wide range of stakeholders. More specifically, it helps to address the wider debate between a "property" and "entity" perspective. The property view was articulated by famed economist Milton Friedman, who held that if a company does anything besides satisfy shareholders, it's forsaking its fiduciary responsibility. The entity view posits that organizations are entities in a broader system and should perform in a way that's consistent with their various communities' values; that CEOs who run companies in ways that are destructive to these values should be "called out." Indeed, many progressive politicians and social activists increasingly are advocating for this entity view.

Leaders, therefore, are caught betwixt and between. Based on most current corporate compensation systems, CEOs are incentivized to focus on performance above almost all else. While increasingly many compensation committees include a "qualitative" performance measurement designed to account for contributions to stakeholder causes, employee workplace satisfaction, and so on, to date it has not become a major differentiator in determining compensation.

Some entity proponents have advocated making a CEO's social action contributions a major compensation factor, but it's unlikely that this will become a widespread reality in the near future. The executive compensation system relies on comparison of similar companies as benchmarks for determining CEO compensation, and it's administered by many prominent HR and comp advisory firms, which decreases the chance that this type of change will happen quickly.

NAVIGATING THE PARADOX: 7 FEASIBLE DIRECTIONS

By definition, paradoxes aren't easy to manage. The notion of holding two seemingly conflicting notions simultaneously in one's head is a prescription for a headache and heartache. For leaders, the temptation is to choose one and ignore the other—for any one critical decision, CEOs wish they could say, "To hell with the trade-off, enough about the stakeholders; I'm going to focus exclusively on shareholders on this one!" This either-or choice isn't possible in today's leadership environment.

Instead, leaders need to pay attention to both sides of the paradox. Here are seven suggestions to facilitate this dual-sided approach:

1. **Live with the frustration.** This may not seem like particularly helpful advice, but CEOs who embrace the tug of war between shareholder and stakeholder groups with much greater equanimity do so to their benefit. The shareholder-stakeholder paradox isn't a problem to be solved; it is a requirement of the role. It's difficult to accept this truth, since most CEOs are solution-oriented, but the inevitable lack of a solution means that no other option exists except embracing this as a given. Leaders have to focus on shareholders at the expense of stakeholders in certain circumstances, and on stakeholders instead of shareholders in others. Therefore, embrace the dichotomy. Recognize that the competing demands aren't going away and that the biggest mistake is to ignore any single stakeholder group. Accepting the frustration inherent in this issue facilitates dealing with it.

2. **Move to a zero-tolerance mindset regarding hot-button issues.** In the old days, CEOs could try and ignore or placate the protests by social action groups, strikes by workers, and other stakeholder tumult, knowing that these problems wouldn't affect shareholders—their ultimate focus. You may recall Bendix CEO William Agee who had an alleged affair with fellow employee Mary Cunningham in the late 1970s into the 1980s. Agee promoted Cunningham quickly to top positions in the company. Though the affair became public knowledge, it didn't have a significant effect on the company's performance, and Agee survived. Today, of course, it would have a huge effect. Witness the McDonald's board's immediate firing of CEO Steve Easterbrook for having a consensual relationship with another employee. Even though Easterbrook had helped the company achieve excellent results, he was fired for what in the past might have been considered a personal transgression. McDonald's board sought to avoid having this minor transgression

have a major impact on businesses—boycotts, negative publicity, plummeting employee morale, and so on.

Zero-tolerance mindset means not allowing yourself or any of your people to engage in behaviors or violate policies that might invite negative stakeholder reaction. CEOs must recognize that they have to be "holier than thou" in an age where they're under constant scrutiny and their actions are communicated instantly and magnified greatly by social media. Similarly, they can't try to brush under the rug what seems like a minor incident, since it's almost certain that employee blogs and other social media will (and for many cases, rightfully), expose it. Every stakeholder group has gained power and influence, and CEOs can and should expect them to use it if they tolerate behaviors to which these groups object.

3. **Find a way to increase your social media awareness and the portal into this environment.** Speaking of social media, you can't ignore it, as much as you might like to. The online chatter about your company can spread virally and overtake you with frightening speed if you're not paying attention. Just about every stakeholder and shareholder group uses Twitter, Instagram, Slack, Facebook, and others, and while some comments about your company may be innocuous, others are not. Any controversy can be blown up; any negative outcome can seem catastrophic.

Therefore, heed the early warning signs of social media negativity. Monitor the online forums and be prepared to respond, both online and with actions, to counteract what's being written. Recognize, too, that analysts are also monitoring the social media threads, and that if they're aware of it, you must be as well.

4. **Create a process to anticipate and respond to whistle-blowers.** It may be an employee complaint about cheating on expense reports or a human rights group that objects to your environmental policies or a customer who exposes a product quality problem. Whatever it is,

you need a process to titrate out the emotionality—to deal with complaints fairly, quickly, and objectively. Just as important, you need this process so that you can defend your actions. Winging it won't work. It's too easy for a stakeholder complaint to slip through the cracks and for some group to rightfully accuse you of inaction on a key issue. A process doesn't guarantee great outcomes on all stakeholder issues, but it does provide a method to deal with the concerns.

Mattel in 2019 received an anonymous letter from a whistleblower claiming the company was underreporting some of their results. Though the stock price dropped when this news became public, it didn't appear to be catastrophic. The company eventually launched an internal investigation and determined the whistleblower was correct—they understated results by close to $200 million—and the CFO departed. If Mattel had a better process in place, they might have acted faster and more effectively when the whistleblower's letter arrived.

5. **Put in measurements for things that can be measured.** When dealing with analysts and others in the shareholder community, CEOs always want to refer to data—they talk in terms of quantifiable increases or decreases to make their points convincingly. Why not follow the same approach when dealing with stakeholders? Admittedly, it's not always easy to quantify business gains relative to stakeholder issues. How do you measure your progress as a good corporate citizen?

Still, you should create measures where you can. For instance, your company reduced your carbon footprint by x percent. Or you closed the gap between your highest and lowest paid workers by x percent. Or you increased the diversity of your workforce by x percent. The numbers matter, giving you a concrete way to communicate your efforts to stakeholders. If you lack a viable means to quantify your progress in a given area, focus on specific activities: forums attended, checks written, charitable events sponsored, and so on. A list of these activities isn't as convincing as specific measures, but it may suffice.

6. **Delegate.** In earlier chapters, I noted that CEOs can't delegate certain responsibilities (such as meeting with an influential senator who is angry about the company's policies, for instance). But when it comes to activities such as creating community outreach programs or reacting to an environmental group's concerns over actions of a subsidiary organization, delegating is an excellent idea. Involving both managers and other employees in these efforts is a win-win: It's effective outreach and good for morale. You can't delegate all tasks when it comes to these types of issues—especially when the issues are controversial and being covered extensively by the media—but you can cherry-pick the ones where delegation makes sense.

7. **Strive to go even further than your own personal value set suggests.** CEOs can easily underestimate what they must do to satisfy stakeholders. They may feel they're making a good faith effort to deal with stakeholder concerns—they've decreased wage disparities, ramped up diversity recruiting, written a big check to a philanthropic group, provided resources for a community program—but often, it's not insufficient. Go beyond what you think is equitable. The standard for stakeholder performance is higher than you think.

EDUCATE, ENGAGE, AND QUESTION

Beyond implementing these seven suggestions, leaders should make the effort to educate themselves and their staffs more fully about the issues of importance to stakeholders. This involves reading about staying at the leading edge of the issues, developments, and events in various areas—cross-cultural, environmental, labor, community, and so on—as well as engaging in discussions with experts in these areas. Knowledge is power. Knowing about an emerging arena of need or concern in a given sector or the actions of a competitor helps leaders avoid being blindsided. Similarly, leaders should engage diversely. Too often, CEOs fail to cross boundaries in their interactions outside of the corporation. They may engage with "the usual suspects"—major customers, other CEOs, heads of trade groups—but they don't talk regularly with academics, bloggers, media commentators, activist groups, and others outside their comfort zone. This broader engagement pattern helps CEOs see the issues they're facing within a larger context, enabling them to prioritize—they're much better able to be big-picture thinkers and figure out mission-critical tasks. Finally, CEOs should encourage their executives to become involved in causes and programs about which they're passionate. This encouragement can be simply recognizing the interest of others—celebrating the efforts of a colleague about a new community program to address homelessness, for instance—or it can involve creating organizational support of a given philanthropic or social action effort. Involvement acts as a counterbalance to the organization's natural tilt toward shareholders—involvement the CEO can point to when someone questions what the company is doing for the greater good beyond making money.

CEOs should also perform regular self-assessments about their performance in these areas. James Manyika, chairman of the McKinsey Global Institute, formulated a terrific list of questions about the changing nature of leadership, some of which are perfect questions for CEOs to use regarding stakeholders. Specifically, here are his four relevant questions:

1. How far do we go beyond shareholder capitalism? How are we accountable to different stakeholders?
2. What is our responsibility to our workforce, especially given future-of-work implications?

3. What is our responsibility for societal and sustainability issues involving our business, and beyond our business?

4. What are our responsibilities regarding participants in our platforms, ecosystems, supply and value chains, and their impact on society?

CREATING A GOOD IMPRESSION

It's not just the facts that people remember but the image that lingers. CEOs can and should communicate their social efforts in statistical terms, but that's not enough. People form perceptions about companies, and if that perception is negative, all the numbers in the world won't change their minds.

Creating an impression is an ongoing activity for leaders. My father had a favorite saying that is apt: "A negative impression cannot easily be changed with more facts—you need to create a different (better) impression." Even organizations with stellar reputations are vulnerable to negative impressions, and these organizations' leaders must counteract these impressions continuously. For years, Johnson & Johnson was seen as a highly ethical and successful organization, and its credo—a statement of beliefs—was considered the gold standard. J&J's handling of the Tylenol crisis in the 1980s (when someone poisoned bottles of Tylenol) reinforced their image as a company that put customers before shareholders.

In recent years, however, J&J has become ensnarled in litigation more than any major corporation, which has left a negative impression on the public. I am sure some on the board will appropriately point out that many of these legal actions are the product of tort lawyers and the rush to class action suits that benefit the lawyers and promote what in the end are frivolous legal actions. Nonetheless, J&J's leaders can't say this in public, as their claims of harassing lawyers and tort lawyers seeking big paydays would appear defensive. The facts don't work here. Instead, the company must strive to create a better impression. One way of doing so is J&J's

CEO becoming a strong proponent of the Business Roundtable initiative advocating addressing the needs of all stakeholders, not just shareholders. Still, they have to engage in more activities of this sort to reverse recent negative impressions.

One company that has done a remarkable job of reversing negative impressions is Walmart. For years, Walmart was accused of exploiting employees by providing insufficient benefits and wages. In recent years, however, the company has made a concerted effort to create a different impression. They have increased wages, offered better employee health care, developed stronger relationships with supplier communities, and changed their board, bringing in more outsiders to counter the insider perception. Not only has the company remained wildly successful and profitable, but it has made a much better impression among various stakeholder communities.

YOUR WORLD IS CHANGING

Leaders know that the world is changing, but it's sometimes difficult to recognize how changes outside the company are affecting policies, programs, and cultural aspects within it. Sometimes their misperception is because they've fallen behind—they don't take social media seriously and fail to follow what people are saying about their company. Or they're in denial about how their company has to change in order to hire the best talent, maintain morale, and meet the needs of the newly evolving social and political challenges.

Whatever the reason, the challenge is to see things as they are rather than how they wish they might be. I worked with the board of a company in which the CEO had been trying to fill a key senior position, and the first woman he hired for the job didn't work out, and then a second woman failed to meet expectations and she resigned. The assumption was that the company had made bad choices in the hiring process and needed to improve its recruiting approach.

When I raised this issue with the CEO and members of the board, we determined the problem wasn't as much the hiring process but rather the prevailing male-dominant culture that had been allowed to flourish. The women executives who had been hired felt uncomfortable in their role and never felt a crucial sense of affiliation with the senior team. With hindsight, we identified small signals indicating that the male-dominant culture was the problem, but at the time the CEO had missed these signals. In years past, women who worked at the company may have tolerated the discomfort. In the wake of the Me-Too movement—and with a drive for diversity among senior executives and the recognition that women with great talent were indeed being passed over—this situation is thankfully no longer tolerable.

The most effective CEOs see these issues clearly and aren't resentful or in denial about how the world is changing. They may not like some of these changes, but they don't let it affect their decision-making as professionals.

I would also disabuse any CEO of the notion that just because he's been successful as a business leader—the company is profitable and thriving—doesn't mean that he's protected from stakeholder-related missteps. Recall the McDonald's and Mattel examples—boards didn't wait long until they punished the leaders who had failed to heed the new social norms.

GOING FORWARD WITH AN AUTHENTIC CAUSE

Organizations can't support every social cause or respond fully and continuously to every stakeholder—they only possess so much time and resources. CEOs need to set priorities and limits. To do so, they should solicit help from their boards. Boards have a lot of skin in this game. When the company performs badly, the board can and should shoulder the blame. In the same way, when the company is sued by a community for polluting their water, the board and the CEO share the blame.

CEOs should adopt causes that are relevant to a company's purpose and products. A defense contractor would gravitate naturally to issues relating to internet security or Washington, DC–based subjects such as privacy concerns. Corning is located in the small, relatively isolated community of Corning, New York, and helped to start a math and science school in the town to supplement the local school system's ability to teach STEM topics. Corning was focused on the quality of education in the region where they were a core player, and thus interests aligned. Corning is a global leader on a wide array of other stakeholder issues, recognizing the value of addressing stakeholder concerns in the larger world as well as in their own backyard.

Here's another not-so-hidden truth: CEOs, for the most part, want to be seen as addressing these dual needs and caring deeply about a variety of stakeholders. In fact, many CEOs resent being chided by analysts and others about becoming involved in various social issue causes. Leaders with whom I've worked are far from heartless. They often are passionate about an issue that affects their organizations—a food company CEO concerned about food availability in central Africa or an energy company head dedicated to the exploration of alternative fuel sources. These leaders don't need to be pushed to become involved—they do so naturally.

The key, of course, is finding the right balance point between involvement and over-involvement. If CEOs can do that, they can navigate the often frustrating path between shareholders and stakeholders successfully.

11

Embrace the Value and Reality of Diversity

A cautionary note: I have focused this conversation around the leadership challenges of setting priorities and executing desired changes to the diversity of senior management teams. This is an important element of diversity and inclusion but only a small part of the larger diversity and inclusion issue.

CEOs I have counseled, taught, or worked with while on the faculty of HBS *say* they are proponents of diversity and the value it brings to corporations. The challenge for leaders is to truly believe what they say and act on these beliefs. We need to ask and assess continuously: Do leaders/CEOs showcase, through their words and behaviors, a genuine belief in inclusivity?

This ongoing challenge is best represented by a typical senior hiring decision. For example, a CEO wants to strengthen the managerial team by adding diverse voices to an executive group. The hiring process brings forward a range of candidates who will expand representation on the traditional senior team. Other qualified candidates are also identified, however, who are likely to make an easier transition into the role but do not broaden the background of the existing team. Immediately, a tug-of-war arises between a CEO's commitment to achieve stated diversity objectives and the potential advantage of hiring individuals with requisite experience who could possibly transfer more quickly into the role. Which candidate does the CEO hire? This is the crux of the issue and where aspirations need to be translated into action if the diversity journey is going to be sustained.

The disturbing truth here is that leaders too often frame the diversity journey as a series of these type of transactional trade-offs rather than seeing each as a part of a broader effort to create a culture of acceptance and change. CEOs often trade off (and privately fret) about how to meet demands for financial returns and achieve strategic/competitive success in a socially conscious manner; they also want to realize all of this in a low-risk, high-return manner while broadening the backgrounds and diversity of their senior staffs.

In private, most CEOs confide that they are upset about their inability to respond faster to diversity mandates. They also wish that their constituents, who want more to happen faster in this area, understood the challenges they face. This frustration is most evident because of the war for talent—particularly for "diverse talent." At a time when the competition for talented executives who can also broaden the diversity of a management team is so fierce, many clamor for those with proven track records. Recruitment is like signing star athletes who are in high demand—finding and attracting them is a major challenge for leaders. All this further complicates the perceived challenge of broadening senior leadership teams.

Another related hidden truth is that not everyone thinks about or even defines diversity in the same way. What diversity means to one CEO may be significantly different from what it means to another leader—or to a board or to an advocacy group. Therefore, CEOs need to crisply articulate what their objectives are and what they seek to achieve, not only for themselves, but also for their boards, employees, and others.

For example, when we think about diversity, we often think about it in narrow terms—in terms of race and gender. Diversity, however, can involve many other factors: socioeconomic upbringing, personal values, philosophies, schools, religious beliefs, and so on. Definitions and clear communications are a critical factor in setting the expectations and agenda for leaders when they speak of needed diversity.

Greater flexibility of approach and creative thinking are also necessary to overcome the "limited degrees of freedom" that some leaders feel constrain them. For example, CEOs can make a conscious effort to significantly broaden the aperture as to the breadth of candidates while they seek to add talent who vary from an organizational norm. One example is John Fish, the founder and leader of Boston's Suffolk Construction, the largest construction company in New England. John has told me that he actively chose to "change the game with recruiting." John believes he can teach people construction business fundamentals more easily than change their thinking processes, and thereby utilize their varying backgrounds. For this reason, Suffolk relies less on lateral hires with construction experience and more on making an effort to hire young liberal arts majors with a wide variety of personal backgrounds who can be trained to know construction fundamentals but who enable Suffolk to have more diversity of thought.

Thus, diversity is a more nuanced set of beliefs and actions in practice for CEOs than it might appear. Unfortunately, we live in a society that increasingly demands instant solutions, and too often, CEOs are compelled to respond with immediate actions that placate the loudest voices rather than offer a lasting solution. It takes courage for CEOs to say, "Achieving meaningful diversity in our organization is going to be a journey, and it will be hard. This endeavor requires perseverance and years of effort."

BEWARE OF REFLEXIVE ACTIONS

Leaders need to balance this need for action with recognition that truly embracing and embedding a culture of diversity cannot be easily achieved by quick, reactionary approaches. Unfortunately, some CEOs respond to diversity objectives this way. It's not that they're being cynical or don't care about the issues, however. They know that certain responses will ease the pressure for action.

This may be why so many leaders appoint an executive in charge of diversity, social responsibility, inclusion, or other words to this effect. While these dedicated jobs/roles are often critically important catalysts for change, the beginning of an effort (and a helpful part of the solution), they are by no means the end point. CEOs need to guard against having others see these appointments as concluding a major part of the journey when in actuality it is the first step in a much longer effort to secure meaningful change. Secondly, the leader/CEO can be seen as "handing off" the diversity issues to the chief diversity officers, even though this is one challenge that can't be delegated away to any one executive. Meeting diversity challenges requires deep introspection and an agile mindset; it means going beyond the scorecards and the tracking that are the starting point of most diversity efforts.

Boards today want and seek minority candidates to fill their openings. According to a recent survey by search firm Spencer Stuart, many of the new board openings are increasingly being filled by those with underrepresented backgrounds. Here, leaders need to avoid the reflex to seek classic candidates—those with varied backgrounds who possess the "right" educational pedigree and "applicable" work experience. It is no wonder boards complain they can't find any candidates—they are thinking narrowly rather than expansively.

What we all must to do is broaden our view. Too often, leaders are relying on search firms that target high-skill, low-risk candidates—"usual suspects"—resulting in a limited group of candidates from which to draw. Ironically, many search firms suffer from the same lack of diversity in their executive ranks as clients; they too are searching reflexively rather than seeking a broader array of candidates who not only are diverse but will add the most value to the company.

Untapped networks, however, exist in just about every industry. These networks need to be developed over time, and when they are, they can provide a vibrant pipeline of new executive and board candidates. Rather than seeking the one individual they need now, more enlightened executive teams will establish and build these informal networks and over the long term establish a wider array of sources for diverse talent.

SIX PROACTIVE ACTIONS

CEOs will find it easier to resist reflexive responses if they approach diversity strategically and holistically. If you're the head of a business, consider the following six actions part of your modus operandi:

1. **Be a believer.** This is as opposed to being a diversity agnostic or atheist. It's not just that this issue isn't going away; it's that given all the value diversity brings to your company and the future of your management team, you must embrace it continuously and genuinely. Seek diversity in various ways—in your board, executive team, and employees, and in your discussions and programs. Seek it not to accommodate the demands of any action groups but in ways that will foster fresh thinking, vigorous debate, and innovative ideas.

2. **Build cohorts.** This word derives from the Roman military term to describe a band of soldiers who were part of a larger legion. In diversity terms, it means thinking about creating diverse, strongly banded groups rather than bringing in a single diversity-satisfying individual. Too often, organizations view diversity from a "single-hire at a time" perspective. But this

is a piecemeal approach to something that needs to be broader and deeper. Too often, CEOs lament the catch-22 of diversity: They want to attract a diverse group of prospective hires, but candidates see that the company isn't very diverse and shy away from working there. Hiring one individual doesn't change this perception. We all want to feel we will be joining a cohort of others like ourselves when we consider where to work. A cohort of "people like me" reassures candidates that they can quickly acclimatize, perform, succeed, and draw others like themselves to their team and company.

Therefore, strive to find ways to build diverse cohorts of management. This is a longer, more deliberate process, but it pays off as the balance of employees shifts gradually and thoughtfully as success in the present lays the groundwork for future success.

3. **Use personal networks.** I don't mean to be negative about executive search firms, but I've found that when leaders tap into their personal networks, they are more likely to find not only diverse candidates for top positions but also candidates who are better able to deliver strong performances. Senior leaders usually have developed numerous relationships with colleagues in different communities and at different companies. It gives them access to a different pool of candidates than possibly the ones available to search firms.

If you're like most CEOs I know, you have substantial relationships with a range of colleagues, business school professors and alma maters, consulting firms, not-for-profit executive directors, community actions groups, and many others. Communicate with them about the types of people you think would be good fits for your company, and the odds are that they will help you surface people of different backgrounds who also are well suited to your organization.

4. **Build a pipeline.** The previous two suggestions—establishing cohorts and tapping into personal networks—are good ways to start creating a pipeline of viable candidates with a range of backgrounds. But you shouldn't stop there. Find ways to have more frequent involvement with those you have come to know and are keeping tabs on. Through continuing outreach, you can increase the odds that you'll have a steady stream of strong candidates applying for all types of roles. This effort can involve inviting potential future candidates to participate in advisory committees that give them insight into the company; you can solicit speaking opportunities that will put you in front of talented gatherings of a wide range of groups (women-in-business associations, minority small business owners, etc.). You also may have SBU (strategic business unit) boards that could provide exposure and opportunities for those in your candidate pipeline where you can get to know them better.

5. **Offer substantive roles.** Be mindful that an appointment to non-operational, largely convening, and limited responsibility roles can signal a limited commitment to real management team diversity. If, however, you can find strong candidates that represent different backgrounds and viewpoints, appointing them to significant positions—senior operating roles, leading a major advisory committee, board members, committee chairs, and so on—makes an impact. They will naturally attract others to the company because of their success in these roles, and ultimately, you create an organic system that supplies the company with a continuous stream of candidates with diverse perspectives and backgrounds.

6. **Do not delegate when it comes to top positions.** Forgive the repetition, but I can't overemphasize this point. CEOs need to be visibly committed to the process. When you reach out personally to candidates and

when you're helping recruit them, you demonstrate to them and everyone else your personal commitment. It's fine to have the CHRO and diversity and inclusion executives involved in aspects of the process, especially when it comes to non-senior leadership positions, but you communicate through your participation that this is an issue that matters not just to you but to the organization as a whole.

What all this boils down to is that CEOs and their senior team must make diversity a priority and realize that this has to be more than just a numbers game. It's not just about having the right percentages of a specific minority. It's not about making a splash with a high-profile diversity hire or launching and publicizing a new inclusion initiative. Today, a war for talent is raging, and the challenge for CEOs isn't just to have a diverse group of executives but to create a culture that attracts those with varying backgrounds, motivates them, retains them, and promotes the best of them to the most senior roles.

While diversity is an essential element from a social/ethical perspective, it helps ensure even greater success from a business leadership perspective. While many CEOs are aware of this truth, they can become frustrated when trying to act on it. The demands on their time and energy are significant and continuous. The varied contextual challenges and the difficult trade-offs that have to be made while trying to expand the quality and diversity of a senior management team are numerous and complex, limiting progress. This challenge is too central to the success of any enterprise to be delegated and the most successful leaders will make the time and find the focus to prioritize diversity for the sake of their communities and the success of the organizations they lead.

12

Know When
to Leave

The analogy with professional sports is apt: CEOs, like coaches, often fail to recognize when it's time to depart. In football, Chicago Bears coach Mike Ditka was lionized after winning the 1985 Super Bowl, but after that season, he was unable to keep the same quality of team talent; the needs of the team relative to the competition also changed, and his leadership soon came into question. He became an anachronistic presence and was fired after 10 years on the job, and his legacy was tarnished. In this same city, Phil Jackson coached the Chicago Bulls to six championships and promptly left after the last one (his desire to depart no doubt intensified by the general manager's desire to remove him). Jackson's legacy was secure.

Many organizational leaders are more like Ditka than Jackson. They enjoy a period of success, receive a great deal of praise, and start to believe that the circumstances that produced these winning seasons can be sustained or duplicated, and they remain. Their success can blind them to changing realities; they don't realize that they're no longer the right CEOs to lead their companies. Perhaps the best, most recent example of this is Jeff Immelt of General Electric. Named by Jack Welch to succeed him in 2001, he enjoyed a lengthy period of success. Then the bottom fell out—major strategy portfolio issues emerged, along with aggressive M&A activity at the tops of markets (power generation and oil field supply), large environmental issues, and continued fallout from the diversification into financial services. The aftereffect of the mortgage-backed securities crisis in 2008 combined with all the other events to catalyze his very public resignation in 2017, with his accomplishments and reputation heavily tarnished. Being CEO for 16 years tempts fate. In a volatile, challenging managerial era, it is far too easy to overstay your time as CEO.

A smaller number of CEOs commit what might be the opposite sin—they leave too soon. Again, like a hot sports coach, they're in great demand, and they see a CEO position as a stepping stone to a better one with a bigger or more prestigious company. They too often do themselves and their companies a disservice. They discover that the adage is incorrect—the grass isn't always greener elsewhere. Though I'll touch on this issue in the following pages, my main focus is CEOs who overstay their welcome.

When leaders know the right time to leave, their companies benefit, and as we have seen through analogy with sports figures, the leaders themselves are also beneficiaries. They depart with their legacies intact and their reputation secured.

It might seem that smart and savvy leaders would recognize that timing is everything. Unfortunately, even the best and the brightest can only see what they want to see. To understand this myopia and what leaders should do to choose the best possible departure dates for themselves and their organizations, we need to explain this hidden truth:

The system is far more critical of CEOs than they believe it to be.

WHAT BOARDS TALK ABOUT WHEN THEY TALK ABOUT CEOs

I've had the opportunity to attend a number of board meetings (and through private conversations with CEOs and board members at HBS and elsewhere, I've also heard many stories about the relationships between the two entities). What might be surprising to many CEOs is that in the executive sessions of board meetings and in the hallway conversations outside and in shared cars on the way to airports, board members talk a lot about CEOs. Equally surprising, these conversations often are more questioning of CEOs' actions than they are celebratory of CEOs' successes. To a certain extent, this criticism reflects human nature—it's easier to focus on challenges than give praise—or at least people seem more motivated to point out wrongs than comment on rights.

But it's also a reflection of the nature of boards. Their mandate is to question, nearly continuously, whether they have the right leader and if this leader is performing well. As a result, their reflex can be criticism rather than applause. I served on a board of a company where we had a high-performing CEO, but even in this instance, we were always discussing if he'd be able to overcome the activist and inherited (from his immediate predecessor) challenges he faced, what additional aid he would need to succeed, and ultimately how long he would or should remain on the job.

I know of a CEO who was operationally brilliant and was delivering wonderful results. Yet, as the markets toughened and competitors grew more emboldened, the board anxiously asked him to articulate and execute a shift in fundamental business strategy. This CEO was uncomfortable with the strategic issues given his laser-like focus on operations. Further, he couldn't see the need to respond to the board's request (given his past success). His attempts at making the needed strategic change were poorly received, and he was replaced. This CEO felt that given his past success, the board would grant him dispensation—that he'd receive additional time to adjust and adapt—and they wouldn't punish him for his discomfort with strategic thinking. Boards, however, aren't concerned just about the present but with the future.

And it's not just boards. To extend our sports analogy, the boards are the owners of the teams, and they have ultimate authority to hire and fire. They possess a certain degree of patience and manage risk/return appropriately. Analysts are akin to the sports media, and they view the coach or the CEO with a far more critical lens and can and do question their every move. Members of the senior executive team are like the players. They have strong opinions and are willing to express them but not for attribution, fearing they'll jeopardize their position on the team. As a consultant, I've interviewed many C-suite executives and other staff about their leaders, and although they're quick to point out the positives, they often include a "but": "Yes, he's terrific with the financials, but when it comes to long-term strategy, well...."

Even the best CEOs have a Damoclean sword hovering over their heads. Some CEOs know this is the case and accept it as part of their role. Some, however, may think they are invulnerable because of their performance or the contextual circumstances supporting their position.

CEOs/leaders have healthy egos—they must believe in themselves to climb to top positions and make tough decisions. At the same time, however, their egos can make them naïve about what people are really saying about them. I know more than one CEO who believes that boards spend the majority of their time discussing all the great things they've done. In reality, boards focus on the missed opportunities and perceived weaknesses.

Some CEOs are in denial. When doing interviews for this book, I would suggest some hidden truths like CEOs not realizing that the system is more critical of CEOs than they believe, and they'd nod their heads and tell me they agree this is true and important to know. But then they'd add, "Thankfully it's not true for me."

Other CEOs can fall victim to the power and influence of their position, and they find it difficult to think of themselves without this influential role. Many leaders relish their supportive infrastructure, the way their days are planned for them, how people are communicating their trust in them and applauding their efforts. The power combined with the pay is seductive.

Most CEOs are also optimistic by nature, and they may recognize that things aren't going so well in the present but believe that a turnaround is imminent. Just as President Hoover said in the early days of the Depression that "prosperity is just around the corner," they believe that their company is one product introduction, one acquisition or market expansion away from reversing their fortunes. Many CEOs have believed their salvation was just around the corner, and it may not happen.

Hubris is also an issue with overlong tenure. Many CEOs are convinced that they and only they can turn around their companies. They may have executed a spectacular turnaround in the past, and they're convinced that they can do it again. Like hope, pride is a great quality, but like hope, it shouldn't be so excessive or unrealistic that it turns into something negative—in this instance, pride morphing into hubris.

Recall the input from Chevron CEO John Watson, whose modesty was a great antidote to hubris. I was congratulating him on the good job he was doing as CEO, and he said, "Yes, I've done a good job, but frankly, when oil prices are high, you look great, and when they're low, you look bad. I understand this, but many of my colleagues who are CEOs don't realize they're being hailed as great leaders only because of favorable external events or the talent of their teams. Instead, they think they're largely responsible for results."

For all these reasons, many CEOs fail to see warning signs that they are in trouble. They're surprised when the discussions that lead to their dismissal commence; they are unaware that the tide has shifted and their tenure is in question. When boards actually get around to dismissing CEOs, these leaders are not surprised because CEO departure requires legal, regulatory, and public relations planning efforts—efforts that are impossible to ignore by even the most tone-deaf CEO. They usually believe they have more time than they actually have. They are convinced that they possess the full and unequivocal support of most board members; that they've been doing a good job; that their stellar record in the past protects them; that they will soon reverse the company's downward trend. They believe all this deeply, and many are shocked when the board starts the process of asking them to depart.

DEPARTURE TIMES AND TYPES

CEOs go through a natural departure evolution based on performance, tenure, and their particular business situations. Some aspects of this evolution can be anticipated while others are the result of business transactions and therefore can't be anticipated. Each stage of this evolution produces different departure issues for leaders. If you're a new and ascending CEO, for instance, your departure context is significantly different from a veteran leader of a struggling business.

Let's look at each of the five stages of this departure evolution and the implications for CEOs:

1. **New and Ascending.** This is the honeymoon period for CEOs. They've been hired usually after an extensive search or at least a great deal of internal deliberation, and they seem ideal for the situation into which they're placed. They may not have carte blanche but usually are given a significant amount of freedom to create and implement strategies. During this time, their future looks bright and their tenure long.

2. **Plateauing/Needing Renewal.** This follows the previous category chronologically. In many cases, something has gone wrong or at least hasn't gone sufficiently right.

After being hired, they often hit the ground running and everything works—for a while. Then the company stays with the strategy too long and plateaus—the continuously upward trajectory goes horizontal. The organization needs a change, a catalyst, a way to move the arrow to the up position. The CEO is on notice—perhaps not officially, but the clock is ticking.

3. **Limited future.** The company is striving for continuous improvement but not doing so fast or far enough. The CEO hasn't renewed the company, and while they haven't yet lost the confidence of the board, they quickly see that they may no longer be the long-term solution. This leader may have a grace period of a year or so but the runway is short.

4. **Face Off.** A business is involved in a major merger transaction—a merger or acquisition—and as a result, two CEOs exist, and a choice must be made. One CEO will win, the other will step out, and boards decide which CEO is in the best position to lead the combined companies. These decisions are almost always negotiated as a central part of the deal initiation and the agreement that follows. There is almost always a known "winner." When US Air and American Airlines merged, as part of the transaction agreement, Doug Parker of US Air was named CEO, and Tom Horton of American was named chairman for a short time (with the expectation he would depart). This happened despite American being the larger of the two companies. If this CEO arrangement hadn't been part of the bargain, the deal probably would have collapsed.

5. **"Walking the final mile."** As the category name implies, these CEOs' days are numbered. Most of the time, they're in this category because their companies have been performing poorly, a scandal has created negative publicity, or for some other reputation-damaging reason. When Boeing experienced well-publicized problems with its 737 Max planes, it became an open

secret that CEO Dennis Muilenberg was leading on borrowed time. Although he seems to have been surprised by his firing, few others were. Carly Fiorina, when she was running HP Compaq, was the recipient of a great deal of criticism after she acquired Compaq and with the manner in which the integration proceeded. Few were surprised when she was released. In last-mile situations, CEOs need to cooperate "with the inevitable".

Besides these five categories, leaders should be aware of organizational needs and whether their skills dovetail with them. Some companies require chief executives who are skilled with transitions—who are adept at facilitating shifts in cultures or at razing traditional organizational structures and moving to flat, team-based ones. These CEOs generally have short tenures—they're like sprinters rather than long-distance runners. They possess a limited time to achieve a known, challenging goal.

Another generalizable CEO/leader role involves the need for scaling. Typically, a company begins its life with an entrepreneur/founder who is great at implementing an innovative concept and takes it through a growth period. This company reaches a point, however, where it needs to grow or die. In these instances, it needs a CEO who is a business expander rather than a founder/creator.

Therefore, understand into which of these categories you fall. Where are you on your path of development and how do your circumstances fit the circumstances in which a company finds itself? Do you still remain the right person for the job, given the evolution of the business and the way you have evolved as a leader? Has the organization plateaued during your watch and are you able and willing to make the changes necessary to restart its upward trend? Is there a natural successor that you have identified and developed and for whom you are now an obstacle to their future development?

Many CEOs fail to ask and answer these types of questions and as a result, end up leaving at the wrong time.

QUICK TO LEAVE, SLOW TO DEPART

Of course, some CEOs leave prematurely, and this is also problematic. Although far more stay too long than exit early, we live in a highly mobile job era, and some leaders see a given CEO position as a stepping stone rather than a capstone. This is especially true in start-ups and entrepreneurial organizations, and younger CEOs take on one top job while eyeing a bigger and better one. The notion of staying and growing with a company is not as prevalent as it once was. The grass isn't always greener, however, and CEOs should consider how a premature departure may hurt as well as help their careers, not to mention their current employers.

Of greater concern is the slow process of replacing a departing CEO. Sometimes, boards move quickly to replace CEOs when the need for change is critical or the business is in serious trouble. Most boards, though, move slowly and deliberately, especially when a problem isn't egregious. Many times, they can live with underperforming leadership for a while. It's also a slow process when a company is lacking internal candidates—moving on from a sitting CEO is a trickier process when an external search has to be conducted or internal candidates need more vetting and grooming.

HOW TO TIME IT RIGHT

It's in everyone's best interest to figure out when is the best time for leaders to leave. Organizations don't want CEOs to overstay their welcome. CEOs who linger too long may be unable to implement the strategies or changes that the organization requires; the skills they possess may no longer be suited to the company they run. Their presence may also drive away the best talent who aspire to be CEO but believe the current chief executive is not going to leave.

More significantly, however, CEOs who stay too long or depart too early hurt themselves—at best they harm their legacy, at worst they exit in disgrace.

Here are some actions leaders can take to get their timing right:

- **Recognize that things likely aren't going as well as you believe they are.** Adopt a self-critical perspective, questioning achievements and your role in setbacks. Be conscious that few leaders enjoy a consistent run of success and acclaim, no matter how many victories they had early on. Force yourself to be objective in analyzing your performance and catch yourself becoming defensive or even worse, being in denial.

- **Embrace the signs of challenge that emerge around you.** CEOs who stay too long often ignore or minimize negative events that occur on their watch. As a result, they're surprised when these events prompt their dismissal. Address the challenges. If you can meet them successfully, great. If not, at least you'll be aware of what's dragging you down, and you can get out before you're submerged completely.

- **Leave them wanting more.** This old show biz adage is applicable for CEOs who have become celebrities in their business sphere. It's always better to depart with your head held high and your accomplishments outweighing your failures. Avoid being the CEO who leaves when the weight of their failures is greater than that of their triumphs.

- **Think about how the timing of your departure will affect your legacy.** Too many CEOs focus on the short term to the exclusion of the long term. Taking the longer view may affect when you leave. If your focus is always the here and now, you won't consider how your decisions today will affect how your CEO tenure is viewed. With a legacy perspective, you'll think twice about remaining in place as things start to unravel.

- **Seek feedback from your board, analysts, shareholders, and others.** Most CEOs hate this recommendation, even though they might not admit it. They don't want to have their performance analyzed by different parties. It's rare for a CEO to say, "Sure, I'm happy to have you interview my team and then let me know what they say." They figure their performance should speak for itself—if the stock is up, if they've met their objectives, then they should be rewarded, and there's nothing needed to be done

- **Find mentors to provide feedback.** Unlike executive coaches who build CEO skills, mentors concentrate on whole individual. Mentors are the ones most likely to tell CEOs that it's time to leave; that if they stay another year, they're going to tarnish everything they've accomplished. CEOs, too, are more willing to trust what mentors tell them than others; they know their mentors don't have agendas beyond helping their mentees.

    Today, CEOs need to be proactive in seeking mentors. They can be former bosses, board members, academics, or industry leaders. As long as they're trusted by CEOs and willing to share tough feedback with them, they can fulfill this essential role.

LOGIC AND INSTINCT

I've known a number of CEOs who managed to leave at the perfect time, and this ability stems from logic and instinct. Logically, their analysis determines that they have reached the point of diminishing returns—that they may have been the ideal CEO before but that changes in the company and the environment will prevent them from enjoying the same success in the coming years. Instinctively, they sense that a change is needed—that voice inside their head tells them that the company needs an infusion of fresh leadership ideas and style.

Two CEOs who left at exactly the right times are Larry Culp and Hubert Joly. Larry was the CEO of Danaher, a Fortune 500 science and technology company. He headed the company from 2001 to 2014, a long, highly successful run. Making astute acquisitions and creating a dynamic culture,

Larry helped Danaher achieve significant growth goals. But toward the end, Larry instinctively understood that he had a spectacular run but that it would be a challenge to continue it in the coming years. And perhaps most significantly, Larry was concerned about the culture he'd created. It was so much a reflection of him that he worried that it would be prevented from evolving organically—that as long as he remained as CEO, he and not the evolving company would determine beliefs and behaviors. Larry departed, taught at the Harvard Business School for four years, and then took on the challenge of becoming General Electric's CEO.

Hubert Joly took over as CEO of electronics retail chain Best Buy when other retailers where struggling because of growing online competition; major competitor Circuit City went under as did other, smaller chains. Hubert led a successful turnaround and resurgence of Best Buy by ensuring its price competitiveness, enhancing the customer experience online and in the stores, partnering with the world's foremost tech companies, and embarking on a growth strategy focused on better addressing the underlying human needs of its customers and that entailed a number of innovative strategies.

But Hubert passed the baton of CEO in 2019, earlier than most people expected. He had three reasons: he felt he had accomplished much of what he had set to achieve when he became CEO; he felt he had built a very strong team, ready and eager to move the company forward; and he thought that the implementation of the growth strategy was off to a strong start but would take a longer time horizon than he felt he had.

I'm sure it was difficult for both Hubert and Larry to leave great companies where they had enormous success, but it was the right thing to do, both for themselves and their businesses.

13

Plan a Post-Leadership Life

I've never been a CEO. Yet I have had the opportunity to help a number of CEOs and other leaders as they exited their roles, and I've interviewed many of these former leaders for this book.

One hidden truth keeps surfacing that is a corollary of the previous chapter—CEOs often don't know when to leave, but when they do depart, they frequently lack a sound plan for life after being a leader. This has negative repercussions for their companies during their departure phase as CEO as well a negative impact on their lives after they exit.

Few CEOs find retirement satisfying initially. The downshift from CEO to former CEO is accompanied by a perceived loss of self-importance accompanied by a somewhat shocking open calendar, decline in emails, and fewer and less weighty meetings. Many CEOs know this is inevitable, but what is most surprising to many is the speed at which it happens. One CEO said to me, "It was inevitable that my calendar would suddenly be devoid of meetings and my emails would fall off. I just wasn't prepared for how fast it happened; it was like the world closed up behind me, and suddenly I was all alone."

The key is determining what are the right post-CEO goals for you. Only when you know this should you begin the process and set expectations around timing to achieve your desired next position or activity.

The decision as to what you want to do has to begin more expansively than narrowly. Most successful CEOs begin thinking about the next era—this is the right time frame for your aspirations.

Is this an era where you see yourself transitioning to another leadership role impacting the lives of many? Not-for-profits, politics, and government service often are destination for CEOs looking to have outsized impacts.

Or is this a time for you to give back to your alma mater and connect with students? In this case, teaching or advisory work with colleges and administration might make sense.

Is this a time to offer wisdom and guidance to others? If so, joining a board of directors and taking on other advisory roles might be your calling.

Do you seek to be an investor, helping to build businesses or turnaround business as an owner rather than as a CEO/employee? Then PE or some form of investing might be what draws your attention.

This level of thinking is a critical and often overlooked first step in the post–CEO departure process. It is very hard to know where you're going if you don't have a heading and a general direction to follow.

Once you have a sense of this direction, the next step is figuring out what your options are.

WHERE DO CEOs GO AT THE END OF THE DAY?

Let's look at some of the most common departure destinations:

- **Academics.** I know about this destination more than most, in part because I left the world of consulting for the Harvard Business School and in part because a number of my faculty colleagues are former CEOs. For some people, this is a great transition. Some CEOs are also gifted, natural teachers, and they love the opportunity to inform and inspire and train the next generation of leaders.

But teaching isn't for everyone. I've seen some CEOs come to Harvard and be shocked by the drastic differences between running a corporation and being in a classroom. As former CEOs, these individuals had to leave behind days filled with flying to varying destinations, worrying about huge numbers of employees and shareholders, making operational and strategic decisions that involved a wide array of executives and advisors, and juggling massive calendar conflicts. As teachers, they have to focus on preparing teaching plans and engaging students.

You go from a showy office with many assistants to a tiny office with no staff. You alone have to prepare teaching plans and create your own PowerPoint slides. Worse, you have entered a land where the "coin of the realm" is academic standing and those with PhDs are the exalted class. A prominent former CEO (who was a terrific teacher) reacted to the sense that he was at the bottom of the hierarchy when, after a particularly difficult day, he came to my office, shut the door, and looked at me and said, "I can only say this to you but … you know, I used to be somebody!" Your prominence as a practitioner will be appreciated, but the *truly valued* in an academic environment, are those that conduct peer-reviewed research and are celebrated by the academy of fellow educators.

This is not an ego-enhancing role. Some former CEOs teach as if they're still running a corporation. They commit the "cardinal sin" of thinking that the class is about them, and they fall into storytelling and advice-giving mode. The reality: Teaching is all about the student, never about you. Instead of focusing on the students and helping them learn and grow, some CEO/teachers focus on themselves.

Students in graduate programs are there to learn through experience and debate—they only want war stories in support of their learning, not for the embellishment of the CEO.

I learned this lesson the hard way. When I left consulting and started teaching at HBS, initially I kept referring to experiences I had had at McKinsey. I did so partially because I thought them instructive, partially because I assumed the stories made me more credible, and truthfully, I figured they would impress the students. Boy, was I wrong. It is a tradition that students at HBS do a comedic roast of their first-year professors on the last day of class. Their roast of me was funny but brutal in its parody of my "McKinsey storytelling and name dropping." Lesson learned. I realized "It's all about the students" that day and thankfully have adjusted my teaching approach since. Unfortunately, some who have become HBS senior lecturers, did not learn this lesson and their impact with students was reduced and their success was limited.

- **Punditry.** Some leaders look forward to life as an elder statesperson and as someone who is called on to opine. They see themselves writing op-eds and blogs, as giving talks, as appearing on shows in which they serve as a fount of wisdom. While technology has made it possible for everyone to have a blog and post comments on social media, it's not the same as speaking from a bully pulpit. CEOs find that the *Wall Street Journal* no longer is interested in obtaining their quotes. Their online followers decrease in number once they're no longer on the job. Many register with speaker bureaus and are surprised to see that unless they were prominent (or slightly infamous) the demand for them and their accompanying fees is low. While some CEOs manage to maintain relevancy because they have a high-profile forum or some other outlet, most find that it's difficult to be an in-demand pundit.

I know CEOs who decide that once they leave their jobs, they'll write books. They say that when they were CEOs, publishers and agents were calling them, almost begging them, to tell their stories. Unfortunately, once they leave office, they are less attractive as authors. Even if they do get published, their books rarely make much of an impact, in part because they're mostly backward looking and largely biographical in content, with wisdom and lessons learned woven into what may often be a disappointing narrative.

- **Boards.** In the vast majority of cases today, a former CEO should not remain on the board of the company that they once led. While a grace period of up to six months for transition and continuity is sometimes granted, it shouldn't extend longer than this period. Boards are well aware that former CEOs cast long shadows and that the new chief executive will rightfully resent operating under that shadow. Boards should make it clear to CEOs that their chosen successor needs to operate in an "open field"; that they shouldn't have to look over their shoulder at the former CEO seemingly questioning their moves and questioning shifts away from existing CEO approaches.

  What is not at all unusual is for CEOs to be a popular choice for other boards after they depart. Unfortunately, this can be a frustrating experience. CEOs have been conditioned to think and act operationally, but boards aren't operators. They see the challenges facing the management team, but they can't directly intervene. The power and influence of boards emanates from three sources: thoughtful probing questions, approval of (often pre-baked and fully vetted) capital and budget plans, and the ability to fire and hire the CEO. Former CEOs as well as any new board members have to operate as counselors, not operators. They are advisory only, and CEOs who transition to boards must make this same adjustment and recognize that it's similar transitioning into an academic role: It is no longer about them. When they become board members, it is about the shareholders and stakeholders they represent.

The other issue is that board work for many companies isn't particularly exciting. As one former CEO confided to me after joining what he thought would be a prominent and exciting board, "You know, this is really quite boring."

Also, sometimes CEOs are invited onto troubled boards because they are seen as sage advisors who can help coach and develop CEOs performing below board expectations. Or, the business is in trouble with investors (or is expected to be) and the board wants members who can be seen as steady hands on the tiller. These situations can devolve, and suddenly former senior leaders and CEO are at the center of a huge storm with limits on how hard they can intervene. They also face personal and reputation threats, and they are suddenly spending excessive time on a board they had hoped would be a place for reflective advice and oversight. Consider the CEOs that were called to help boards such as Uber, Boeing, Valeant, J&J, VW, Wells Fargo, and Facebook to name but a few recent examples.

- **Private equity investing.** Some CEOs leave companies with dreams of turning their operation and strategic prowess into investments and making outsized returns as they leverage their expertise in private equity firms. In reality, most private equity partners don't really need or want another partner, especially in environments when there are too many investors and not enough deals. For instance, the current one that has been created by the huge run-up in valuations in 2019–2020 followed by the collapse caused by the COVID-19 crisis. Also, the hard truth is few CEOs are great investors. PE partners are highly skilled at seeking deals where leverage and operational expertise can be applied to strategic assets that are often poised for growth or need intervention to garner returns. This is a skill that is built over many years and many deals (and many failures). CEOs tend to think more operationally and less as financial engineers, and while some become skilled deal makers, many do not. Private equity partners want new partners who also bring deals with them—few CEOs have the networks and affiliations that PE players have to produce a string of new PE possibilities.

- **Running a smaller or a different type of business.** Some former chief executives move to the not-for-profit sector, convinced that they can use their knowledge and skills in the service of others. The challenge: Leading a not-for-profit is nothing like leading a for-profit corporation. The former has employees who don't really want to be led; most of the people are passionate about the cause and relish a collaborative environment. They have little interest in hierarchical decision-making. All this isn't to say that CEOs cannot become wonderful leaders of mission-driven entities about which they're passionate, just that they should understand that they can't "lead" them as they did their former companies.

- **Consulting.** Some CEOs decide that their departure gives them the chance to become consultants. The problem with being a consultant is that CEOs are used to telling people what to do, and consultants only advise people what they might do. It's a huge difference, and it can be extremely frustrating for a CEO who feels advising is a weaker and less powerful role.

- **Becoming an entrepreneur.** Creating a start-up might seem like a good idea to some former CEOs, but it too comes with a lot of adjustments. Working with a small staff and limited resources can be difficult if you're accustomed to large teams of people at your beck and call as well as sizeable budgets. As one former CEO who created a start-up told me, "I used to have this big, beautiful office in Silicon Valley with this gorgeous view. Do you know that now I sit in a bullpen with others half my age and I am preparing my own PowerPoints for capital raising meetings that are slightly embarrassing for me to have to attend!"

I'm not trying to discourage CEOs from choosing any of these options—as we'll see, they are viable options if they meet certain personal criteria. But I would be remiss if I didn't issue fair warning that the transition can be rocky. Before looking at how to create a plan that not only makes the transition less rocky but also helps turn it into a tremendously satisfying second act, let me focus on why leaders should have a plan in place long before they depart.

WHY EXIT PLANS MAKE SENSE FOR LEADERS AND THEIR BOARDS

Creating a plan for post-CEO life is difficult for CEOs caught up in their demanding jobs, but a general plan is essential to making a seamless transition and, as such, creates a much better situation for both CEOs and their companies. When you have a finish line, you can stride toward it confidently and with purpose; you know what you want and need to accomplish before departing. You perform better in your job because your objectives are clear and time sensitive. You feel better because you're not fretting about your upcoming transition into uncharted territory. And your board feels better because they are reassured by the reasonable time line you've laid out.

Some CEOs, however, become so enmeshed in the details of their daily work lives, they find it hard to think about what comes next. Some will rationalize that they are working to the final day with appropriate energy and commitment. Some don't want to tell the board definitively when they plan to exit and what they plan to do because articulating it makes it real.

Recognize, though, that even if CEOs don't create a post-CEO plan, their boards are contemplating this issue.

This is especially true when CEOs have reached a certain age or tenure. As I've stressed, boards always want (and need) a succession plan in place.

Leaders must accept the reality, too, that their departure plan probably won't likely include a new CEO role. There are a number exceptions to this statement, of course. Some people are specialists—turnaround CEOs who are brought in for relatively brief time periods to reverse a business's course. In this instance, they probably will be in demand and may have another CEO position on the horizon. There are also people who are in mid-career and climbing a ladder of CEO positions that have escalating prestige and responsibility. But for many chief executives, the plan will not include another top job. And, frankly, few want to put themselves through the same grind after enjoying sustained success in the position. Successful CEOs, no matter how smart or talented, understand that a significant amount of their success was due to having the right team, situation, and assets in place and a substantial dose of good luck. Why risk their legacy on another CEO position where everything is unlikely to align so neatly for them?

Many CEOs get one big chance at leading a company, and if they're lucky, they make the most of it, staying 8 or 10 years or even longer. At a certain point, they peak, and even if things don't go downhill, they are highly unlikely to reach this peak again. Everyone can see that their time on the job is coming to an end. Facing it with a plan is a much better option than facing it without one.

HOW TO FIND THE RIGHT POST-CEO PURSUIT

There's no one-size-fits-all departure plan for CEOs. What's right for John may be completely wrong for Mary. As much as I may make light of CEOs who believe that golfing 24/7 represents an ideal post-CEO plan, it may be perfect for some people. I've found, however, that most CEOs are intellectually active, highly engaged individuals who relish challenges and remaining relevant. For them, the golf course isn't the place that will provide them with these outcomes.

The following plan suggestions, however, might lead them to a highly satisfying post-CEO life:

- **Have a passion and follow it.** Is there something you've always want to do or something that you believe deeply in that you've always wished you could be more committed to? Let that be a guide for what you consider doing next. I know a former CEO who has always been passionate about the challenge of climate change and has spent nearly his entire post-CEO life lending his time, money, strategic expertise, and managerial abilities to creating awareness of this issue. Another is passionate about collecting cars and spends a lot of his time traveling around the country attending car rallies and buying and selling vintage vehicles. A third is a fly fishing addict and travels around the world finding new streams and rivers where he can practice his art.

  It matters little what the passion is—it can be related to previous business skills or involve not-for-profit work, or hobbies. It can involve starting a new company, joining an existing enterprise, or doing something on one's own. But it offers ex-CEOs engagement and challenge, which is what all leaders/CEOs need as they step away from a demanding CEO/leadership role.

- **Share what and who you know.** The "who" is likely to be the critical piece of this suggestion. CEOs generally have terrific networks built up over years of interactions with a wide variety of professionals—business leaders, consultants, academics, and others. Providing access to these networks is a way of giving back and remaining relevant. Sharing who you know can take many forms. You can mentor young people who are just getting started in their careers. You can teach. You can consult. You can do pro bono work. You can join associations and other groups that help everyone from small businesses to cause-focused activists. This isn't about lecturing others about how they should do things or telling endless war stories from your time as CEO. You don't want to be the old person sharing stories and your opinions (which is often viewed as a slightly veiled attempt to criticize others). Rather, be generous with the resources you've accumulated, helping those who need your help. Responding to requests for ideas and contacts can be tremendously satisfying for former CEOs. They've accumulated a lot of both, and they have the opportunity to distribute them to those who value their resources. Leaders have healthy egos, and this sharing helps enhance and feed a greater sense of self, not ego.

- **Be disciplined about how and when you implement your plan.** CEOs tell me that they've received a range of advice about *when* to start the work after leaving as CEO. In fact, one CEO for whom I have a lot of respect, nonetheless gave me highly questionable advice. He advised that when I left consulting, I should wait a year before deciding what to do next, his premise being that I needed to listen and think about lots of possibilities before making a decision. It's poor advice because this is a process that requires considerable time but not all your time. It is best done gradually. I always advise leaders nearing the end of their tenure to talk with many others and, importantly, try on the roles that others are playing or advocating. "Wear the idea" for a week and ask yourself how would this feel? Would I be fulfilled? What would others think of me if I played this role well? Then have another conversation and ask yourself the questions again. If you wait until you have a lot of free time, the fear of the "empty calendar" will become increasingly challenging. The inability to articulate "what's next" when everyone asks will become uncomfortable. Start this process well before you are ready to leave.

Let me also share some great advice I received from McKinsey's former managing partner Ron Daniel. I was about one year from my retirement date when we sat down together over lunch. I asked him when I should begin planning my post-retirement life, based on his experience of counseling many McKinsey senior partners and CEOs and other leaders in transition. His first words were, "You are late." He told me that "this is a process and requires time, discipline, patience, and a reflective effort—ideally you would take two years to do it well." Second, he recommended, "You need to have an office out of the home." When I expressed skepticism about this being a core recommendation, he elaborated: "You can't work from home if you want to be relevant." He stressed the value of being surrounded by colleagues, even if they didn't work directly with me. He believed that the ability to have work-related conversations and engage in an ongoing dialogue with others about new ideas and approaches is crucial. He noted that we shared a number of colleagues, and he had knowledge of many clients who had retired and told him that they'd work from their "Florida office," which turned out to be their second home. Most ended up playing golf or sailing, doing part-time investments (which turned out to be mostly managing their personal portfolios and talking to others about small investments), and atrophy set in quickly.

Ron also advocated attaching yourself to a knowledge-based institution or finding a learning-oriented environment. This means staying close to the ongoing stream of information and ideas. At consulting firms such as McKinsey and at law firms, think tanks, and other associations, this knowledge is being exchanged continuously, and those who are there benefit from exposure to it. They are aware of new trends, emerging markets, and cutting-edge innovations. This awareness helps people feel relevant. Finding a place that helps you "remain current" helps avoid the risk of, as Ron so eloquently put it, "withering on the vine."

- **Don't chase dollars.** If you haven't made your money previously, it is unlikely you will "make it" after you leave. Some CEOs end up chasing money. They're on speakers' bureaus charging large sums for a speech or they're chasing memberships on big corporate boards that pay at the top of the range for directors. CEOs who chase dollars are rarely rewarded financially, and they risk losing self-esteem and having little impact. Be driven by your passion, not dollars.

- **Leave your legacy to others.** I know that CEOs are often worried about legacy issues, but it's out of their control. You can't spend your time trying to write—or rewrite—your history. You need to avoid being defensive and producing op-eds and blogs that thinly hide the fact that you're defending your decisions as CEO. Don't engage in debates with people about what occurred under your watch. What's done is done. As an Italian client summarized as only Italians can: "Get in the retirement car, and rip off the rear view mirror because what is behind you is of no concern."

TWO EXAMPLES: A GOOD AND BAD POST-DEPARTURE EXISTENCE

Daniel was the CEO of a well-known company who had a lot of success over the course of his eight years there. He was a competent leader but also a self-important one who claimed more credit for the company's success than he possibly deserved. When the business started to experience problems, he departed abruptly and without a plan—it was as if he didn't want the emerging problems to taint his legacy. During the first year after he left, Daniel wrote a book about his management philosophy. Not only didn't it sell as well as he had hoped, but it was obvious to those "in the know" that he was inflating his accomplishments—and many thought he did so in order to preserve his legacy. Daniel also involved himself in some philanthropy, but the charitable institutions where he was involved felt he was a "dabbler" and never viewed him as a serious proponent of their causes. Nonetheless, he often offered these groups unsolicited advice—advice they rarely followed. Daniel also lobbied for membership on a major corporate board, and he was appointed to it. Although it wasn't cause and effect, the company went downhill shortly after he joined, and Daniel was constantly criticizing the company's strategy and policies, earning the ire of the CEO and other board members even as the business declined and was eventually sold to a competitor.

Martha's post-CEO journey was significantly different from Daniel's. First, she started planning her departure more than 18 months before she was ready to leave, and she informed her board early on about her intent and actively and thoughtfully helped them with the succession planning. When Martha departed, her business was flourishing, and the board and the new CEO were highly supportive and grateful for all the positive things she had done for the company. A close family friend had an oldest son who was a young tech entrepreneur working in Silicon Valley, and he was running a start-up that had great products but lacked business expertise. The young man had been calling her regularly for business advice, and when Martha told him that she was going to step down, he asked that she become a consultant to his start-up—a request that she was happy to grant since she'd always been fascinated by the culture and companies of the burgeoning start-up universe. She moved to Silicon Valley in part due to the start-up and in part because of a long-planned move to the West Coast. There she split her time between the start-up office and a not-for-profit on whose board she had served previously. Besides her board duties, Martha served as a mentor to the not-for-profit group's executive director, helping her implement a growth strategy designed to forge alliances with others in the sector as well as create alliances with corporations aligned with their mission.

The stark contrast between Daniel's and Martha's post-CEO existence demonstrates the value of leaving in a thoughtful way—with a plan, a passion, and a place in mind.

14

Strive for
Authenticity

CEOs believe themselves to be authentic leaders. Why would they not? Who views themself as a leader of others but perceives themself as a pretender, actor, or placeholder?

Leaders strive to be true to their beliefs and their ideals. Unfortunately, the role of CEO exerts a powerful influence on how they ultimately choose to lead and manage. It isn't until they're in the core leader role and faced with the realities of day-to-day leadership (many of which have been detailed in this book) that the desire to be "true to oneself" is tested. Too often, new leaders arrive in their roles with lofty expectations of what they can accomplish and how they can accomplish it. I have detailed the many challenges to taking and sustaining action as a CEO. *How* a leader chooses to achieve their outcomes is equally challenging. CEOs arrive with a vision of themselves as commanding in their leadership style, involving others in an equitable and collaborative manner, making key decisions after thoughtful debate, and ultimately driving a collective effort to great results. These expectations are often dashed by harsh realities.

Indeed, the hard truth is that new CEOs arrive on the job and struggle to meet these lofty and often unattainable leadership style aspirations and may quickly find themselves acting a part rather than being genuine. In this way, they fail to be authentic leaders.

Suddenly, the reality of the role and strategic, operational, managerial, and stakeholder and constituent challenges force CEOs to abandon their personal desire to be true to themselves. Leaders may believe themselves to be authentic, but their actions say otherwise. They allow the role to dictate their style and substance rather than the other way around.

THE GENUINE ARTICLE

The HBS faculty member and also former CEO of Medtronic, Bill George, defines authentic leaders as individuals who are genuine and true to their beliefs. They lead with consistent values and with their heart as well as their head. George, who has written extensively about this concept, posits five dimensions to authentic leadership:

1. purpose/passion;
2. values/behavior;
3. relationships/connectedness;
4. self-discipline/consistency; and
5. heart/compassion.

George's concepts frame a major course at HBS that he and Professors Tom Delong and Scott Snook have taught students and executives about how to identify and sustain their authentic leadership styles. This course, Authentic Leadership Development (ALD), is immensely popular. Students seek ways to identify what is authentic for them, and how to sustain this authenticity given the challenges of not only leadership in business but also the challenge of life as well.

ALD's key dimensions are a useful set of lenses through which you can identify what constitutes authenticity and inauthenticity. As a CEO, you can judge authenticity in part by asking yourself if your staff are willing to be open and forthright when you engage them in conversation. Assess the following critically: Are they reticent to tell you bad news; do they make excuses or try to avoid sensitive topics; will they push you and push topics that may not please you? When people consistently behave this way in your presence, they're usually modeling your behavior—if you're authentic in truly wanting and asking for openness and transparency, they'll respond in kind.

Another sign of authenticity is assessing how staff and executives interact with you: Are they relational rather than transactional; does your staff confine themselves to job specifics during conversations? If so, they will focus on numbers and facts—delivery dates, percentages, dollars, percentage completed, and so on—to the exclusion of broader contextual elements that underlie the results. A relational conversation includes the specifics but also leaves room for context and a broader assessment of what lies behind the specifics. It should also include questions about personal opinions. Ideally, a truly relational talk would touch on personal and family issues and be leavened by humor and warmth.

Authentic CEOs enjoy two-way rather than one-way conversations. Many CEOs leave meetings with colleagues and comment afterward that "we had a really good conversation." In truth, if a tape were made of the conversation and replayed, it would often reveal that the CEO dominated the conversation. Many executives have said about such interactions, "They (the CEO) sucked all the oxygen out of the room" or that "it was a lecture disguised as a conversation." CEOs often assess these conversations inaccurately. They are so accustomed to seeing these interactions through the decision/transactional lens, they fail to look at the same interaction through the authenticity/relational lens. Their perspective would shift if they changed lenses. Authentic leaders are able to engage in real dialogues rather than monologues disguised as dialogues. They can actually alter beliefs and change mindsets through inquiry-based questions and conversation. When they do suggest action that can explain the "why" of strategies and decisions; they connect the larger concepts back to individuals and their responsibilities.

In fact, leaders can communicate in this holistic manner without saying anything. The way they sit, when they choose to have an interaction, the expressions on their faces—all are part of an authentic dialogue.

One of the key learning sessions we do at HBS focuses on the importance of communication and communication styles; it features a filmed case of two executives going through their day working at the same company as co-CEOs. We ask participants to suggest criteria for what makes a great leader. We capture these criteria, and then we ask the participants to critically view the videos and assess the individuals based on what they have seen.

At the end of the case, participants are forced to confront the fact that they made all manner of critical and highly evaluative judgments about these co-CEOs based on observation of their interactions alone. Through the exercise, they are able to view interactions through a third-party lens. This provides insights about how leaders communicate in meetings and lunch rooms as well as hallways. As a result, participants draw all manner of conclusions as to the quality and substance of a leader. The participants are surprised at the end of class when they are challenged to think about how others have been viewing them in the same manner.

We use this case to showcase two additional crucial learnings. After we ask them to vote on which of the two executives should be named the sole CEO (the outcome vote is always about evenly split between the two filmed executives), participants are shown their previous criteria and discover that they didn't use any of their formal criteria in these assessments of CEO readiness. Rather, they focused on the softer, more "authentic" elements of the co-CEO to make their judgments. Second, they realize that the "authentic" behavior they observed drove their opinions of the co-CEOs, not the actual decisions and the content of the co-CEOs' activities.

The point: How you take action and lead daily (and not only those actions you execute) affects how you are viewed as a leader—the perception is based on a complete set of behaviors. Many argue that the "softer," more authentic elements of how people manage are the defining characteristics for failure or success as a leader. The rationale is that if you are unable to get individuals to be committed, to believe in your planned actions, and to follow you, then you are not a true leader.

These more relational elements and personal attributes create the authenticity that is unique to you and which, by definition, takes many forms. When CEOs act like themselves, they allow their personalities to shine through, so a range of leadership styles can be authentic. Some lead with evangelical passion, others with disruption, still others with quiet confidence. Therefore, don't expect that one particular leadership style or method is the only way to ensure leadership success.

In an earlier chapter, I emphasized how humility is a valuable trait for leaders. Again, I am reminded of another piece of advice from Ron Daniel, McKinsey's former managing director. Ron was asked his perspective by a large group of newly recruited associates in an initial training session on "how to be successful at McKinsey." He demurred but did offer a broader observation on leaders and success more generally: "Take the high road to success. It is paved with humility and it is far less traveled."

Ron was reminding the new associates that authenticity and humility go hand in hand. If you're comfortable being yourself, you will not feel the need to boast and set yourself above and apart. You will naturally use your own humility to draw others to you—a necessary trait for all successful leaders. The "high road" part of the advice has to do with being a professional and never violating the ethical or professional boundaries of one's leadership—another important piece of advice.

HOW DO YOU MEASURE YOUR AUTHENTICITY?

Admittedly, this isn't always easy. Whether CEOs rationalize how they're behaving or they're in denial about it, most always believe they're being genuine. So it's not enough to ask, "Am I being authentic today?"

We can, however, assess our daily actions and obtain a sense of how they make us feel. Do our daily tasks seem natural and comfortable or do they feel artificial and uncomfortable? To illustrate, suppose Tina is a CEO who is naturally friendly and loves soliciting ideas and information from a wide range of people. She relishes modeling behaviors that she believes are consistent with the organization's values. When Tina has to spend an entire day in her office on process concerns and administrative calls, it feels wrong, and she feels discomfort; she's not allowed to be her naturally gregarious self. She feels constrained by her circumstances. When Tina is out and about, interacting with a wide range of individuals, asking questions and listening hard to answers, she feels like her best, truest self.

Another measure: Ask yourself how aware you are of the effect you're having on people with whom you're interacting. Inauthentic leaders generally find this question unnecessary or of limited value as they are more focused on the quality of their one-way conversations and wonder whether their messages were received and understood. Authentic leaders care how they're affecting people. They ask themselves, "How am I being experienced?" While they're speaking, they ask themselves if they are noticing a lifted eyebrow, a slight smile, a nodding head, a sudden shift in posture as listeners lean forward to hear more of what is being said. Authentic leaders are gifted listeners. Such listening includes involving all your senses as you measure and "feel" the effect you are having on others.

A third assessment: Determine whether people are responding to your leadership as a collective rather than as a group of individuals. Authenticity draws people together.

Is the group of individuals who received the initial message or assignment now a group of committed team members driving to a common objective? Have you interacted, challenged, and engaged this assemblage in such a way that they are drawn together and carry forward together? Among the greatest gifts of an authentic leader is the ability to motivate an individual to work as a collective aspiring toward a common objective.

PITFALLS: HOW INAUTHENTICITY HAPPENS

A predetermined sense of what a role should entail is a powerful catalyst for inauthenticity. If new CEOs find themselves adhering to standard routines, believing predictability ensures tasks are defined and executed, they will struggle to be perceived as authentic. Employees want to see CEOs who are engaging in, reacting to, and feeding off the energy and ever-evolving needs of the staff, the business, and the broader community. They want improvisation as well as routine. They need a leader who reacts in real time to real impulses. A flexible and responsive managerial approach conveys authenticity; reliance on routine and repeatability of effort does not.

Some CEOs are inauthentic because they believe themselves to be great actors. They think that playing the part of the determined leader will help them succeed as CEO. They are certain they can sell others on their CEO persona, inauthentic as it may be. My colleague Scott Snook talks about how people have an innate and uncanny ability to sense authenticity in a leader. Scott references the old "scratch and sniff" advertisements that used to be in magazines as a metaphor as to what individuals do every time they interact with a new leader. They "scratch and sniff" that individual to quickly determine the degree of comfort and connectedness the leader is exhibiting.

Indeed, some leaders seek CEO positions primarily for personal affirmation or ego gratification. Secretly—or not so secretly—these individuals relish the spotlight and the adulation that can come with the job. CEOs have healthy egos, but authentic leaders don't aspire to the job for ego alone. They genuinely want to help others in the company succeed, knowing that if they achieve this objective, they too will succeed. They want to build something, to leave a company better off than before they arrived. CEOs who are inauthentic and simply want to be lavished with praise will soon find that they are no longer leaders since no one is drawn to follow them.

Another pitfall for inauthentic leaders is sending signals that they only really want positive feedback. As I've noted earlier, some leaders make sure that their people know to tell them what they want to hear rather than the truth. Inauthentic leaders often make it known—directly or indirectly—that they expect feedback that reinforces their view of themselves.

On a number of occasions, I've listened to a major speech by a CEO, and when they finish, they approach their staff and advisors (like me) and ask, "How did it go?" At that moment they truly want to hear positive feedback, which is understandable. Authentic leaders know enough to wait a bit, so they and their teams can reflect on what was said. Only then do they ask their teams again: What was the reaction to the speech? This time, they want real feedback. They're sufficiently astute to realize that no one is going to be completely honest with them right after a big talk. Authentic CEOs know that the most valuable feedback arrives in one-on-one meetings with a trusted colleague an hour or two or day or two after the event.

Finally, a common pitfall for inauthentic leaders is assuming that verbal agreement equals conviction. People agree with CEOs reflexively. They have transactional conversations in which they respond affirmatively to the CEO's ideas and requests. Authentic leaders realize, however, such affirmation and agreement is often superficial. To secure genuine conviction, they need to develop a deeper relationship—one that my widely celebrated Harvard colleague Tom Delong refers to as a "covenant," that is based on a personal commitment to one another rather than a mere transaction.

HOW TO COMMUNICATE AUTHENTICALLY

As I've noted, authenticity means trusting your inner self to drive the sense of who you are, allowing your true beliefs and personality to emerge instead of "playing the role." This is easy advice to give but challenging for many CEOs to follow comfortably. The biggest authenticity challenge often involves communications.

Here are suggestions for how to communicate authentically:

- **Show humility.** You may be tired of my emphasis on humility, but it's a secret weapon of successful CEOs. Leaders sometimes engage in tough conversations for which they feel unprepared. Typical CEO behavior is to be boldly assertive, not really acknowledging that they don't know something or that they are feeling uncomfortable by new and challenging material. An authenticity-based approach means acknowledging your discomfort. Own the fact that you might not fully understand what is being discussed or outlined. Watch how people respond. They will see that you are humanizing yourself, are open to getting help, and being solicitous of others, and people will be drawn to help you. All by showing a bit of humility. Remember it is a "road not well traveled."

  Being empathic and humble isn't an act. You have to mean it; you have to make an effort to discard the personality traits you think a CEO should have and respond to situations genuinely, as you might to a friend or loved one.

- **Talk less and listen more.** You don't just have to speak authentically to communicate in this manner. In fact, when CEOs dominate the conversation, they often come across as inauthentic pontificators. When you probe and listen more and talk less, you learn a lot more and also communicate a sincere desire to know another person's ideas. Open-ended questions and managed silences serve CEOs well.

- **Measure other people's communication.** One measure of your impact as an authentic leader is whether others are emulating your approach. Assess if others are also speaking authentically. Are people emulating your genuine communication style? Ideally, the effect is like a line of falling dominoes—one person after the next adopts an authentic way of conversing. When you empower others to be authentic, you're doing something right.

- **Tailor your remarks.** Audiences want to be spoken to in a manner that is designed to communicate to them specifically, not some broader group. In the moment, they want you to address their particular issues. Even a large group wants to feel you are speaking to them as individuals. To do this, avoid the stump speech and find a way to make bespoke remarks as much and as often as possible.

- **Rehearse your formal remarks.** A trap is failing to rehearse when making more formal remarks/speeches. Most leaders hate rehearsing. Yes, it takes time, and some CEOs believe that they've given so many presentations/formal talks, they don't need rehearsal or that they can just read from a script. But rehearsal facilitates authentic communication. By rehearsal, I'm suggesting focusing on what you want to communicate and how to make it meaningful to a given audience. Practice the key points you want to make in front of someone who knows this audience well and who you trust to provide honest feedback. What does this person think of your perspectives? How will they be received? Are they tailored enough? Again, rehearsal isn't about memorizing a script; it's about making yourself more comfortable with the message and themes you want to convey and doing so in a manner that the audience will hear.

HONESTY WORKS

Here's another hidden truth related to authenticity: People respond positively to sincerity and candor, no matter what's being said.

In a culture where people feel leaders are not completely truthful and that a gap exists between leaders' words and deeds, honesty is greatly appreciated. For example, it was reported that when Reed Hastings, Netflix's CEO, decided to split his company into two, one for DVD delivery and the other for online streaming, investors and consumers reacted negatively. Hastings reversed his decision, and when he did so, someone asked him how it felt to apologize for a business mistake. He responded that after going through marriage counseling, he had learned the value of honesty, both in his personal and professional lives. He discovered that if you are sincere, people greatly appreciate honesty, even if it isn't what they want to hear.

15

Seek Truths
in the Future

The 14 hidden truths discussed in the 14 earlier chapters aren't going away. In fact, they are likely to be even more relevant in the future than they are today. In a world that is becoming increasingly complex, volatile, global, and digital, we need these truths more than ever before—truths about authenticity, cooperation with boards' fiduciary and ethical oversight, and diverse perspectives on the wide variety of operational leadership challenges. In quickly changing environments where every moment and each decision counts, CEOs need to hit the ground running and not be blindsided by the unexpected requirements of their new leadership roles.

Today, many new CEOs are surprised by what their job involves. In the future, they may be shocked—shocked to the point that they struggle to deal with the time demands, required skills, and limited talent, as well as a lack of available capital. For this reason, leaders need to prepare themselves for the job's increasing degree of difficulty—not just obvious challenges but those that reside beneath the surface.

PREPARE FOR GROWING DEMANDS

Earlier we examined constituency consciousness, and while the difficulty of balancing stakeholder demands in 2020 is intense, it's going to become even more intense as a new wave of constituents crests. Take climate change. Invariably, this is going to become an even more pressing issue for businesses in the coming months and years—we're going to see external special interest groups and internal concerned corporate citizens demanding that companies not only reduce their carbon footprint but become far more active participants in addressing the causes of climate change. We're also going to see increasing globalization of business as the digital divide abates and information and markets flow ever more unconstrained across national borders. Capital markets will become even more international as stakeholders in Shanghai, Vladivostok, and Buenos Aires become just as invested in US business performance as stakeholders in Dallas, Atlanta, and Cleveland. Learning to manage time and resources in the face of all these stakeholders clamoring for attention will be a major challenge for leaders.

Similarly, CEOs should be prepared for growing pressure to change management. Jack Welch's suggestion that "the best way to enact change management is to start by changing the management" is going to become increasingly relevant. As new markets emerge, customers evolve, and technology advances, businesses need to match these changes with new and more talented executives. And in most instances, CEOs will have to make changes even faster than in the past to win what has already become a global war for diverse talent. Earlier I discussed the allure of slow change, and no doubt this allure will remain in the tumultuous times ahead. Speed, however, will be of the essence as social media sends new information out globally and instantly and as technology fosters even greater organizational transparency. CEOs will have to respond to all types of questions, problems, and opportunities in hours or days rather than weeks, and this applies to management change especially.

Another hidden truth—that it's lonely at the top—isn't going away. It stands to reason that as competition intensifies, as CEOs incur ever increasing demands and face more challenging board requirements, and as social media creates unprecedented amounts of transparency, many leaders will feel the increasing degree of difficulty of the CEO leadership role. Invariably, many will feel less understood as even fewer appreciate the reality of their roles. They will remain isolated and without peers and counselors who can ensure that they are told the whole truth and from whom they can obtain sage and objective counsel.

Although all the truths discussed will remain factors in the coming months and years, the one about CEOs hearing only partial truths will be particularly relevant. Recall my earlier story about the Navy admiral who, upon arriving on his aircraft carrier's bridge, know only two things with certainty: that he'd never be handed a cold cup of coffee and that he would not be told the whole truth. In tense, confusing times, telling the unvarnished truth takes more courage than many may be able to muster. Employees, managers, and C-suite executives will be further challenged to overcome the natural desire to please and will be reluctant to convey all the bad as well as good news.

Now and in the future, CEOs must be like the admiral and recognize that they need to accept and plan for never getting the full picture easily.

RECOGNIZING NEW REALITIES

As the bar is raised on CEO performance, leaders must be aware of the 14 hidden truths to clear this bar. Awareness of these truths gives CEOs a better understanding of one of the most difficult jobs in the world. This understanding helps leaders assess their situations realistically and determine the optimal ways to spend their time and the skills that are most important for the situations they face.

Recent events make this point abundantly clear. As of this writing—entering the eighth month of a global pandemic—everyone from business leaders, academics, health care professionals, public servants, media, investors, and all manner of stakeholders have suddenly been forced to experiment with and gain proficiency using the digital tools required to work remotely. CEOs are receiving a crash course is distance leadership, attempting to communicate and motivate effectively through digital means/screens. As a professor, one day I was surrounded by 90 students in the famous Harvard Business School tiered classrooms, and the very next week I was seeing them as a bunch of small, stacked images, much like the title sequence of the Brady Bunch television show. In the classroom, I could no longer respond to their body language and expressions, I could not "feel" how students reacted to one another or how much they were learning as a group. Online, the world is reduced to two dimensions, and with it the loss of a sense of connectedness, emotions, and understanding that comes from human interaction. Like educators around the world, I have been changing the way I "read" student reactions to assess how I educate.

Leaders face far more challenging adjustments than simply working in this remote fashion. CEOs need to orchestrate problem solving, teamwork, shared exploration, and innovation as well as create followership across a wide variety of stakeholders and constituent groups. The post-pandemic environment will bring massive new challenges and many new changes to what is already a immensely difficult leadership role.

If CEOs are unaware of the hidden truths—if they think full transparency accompanies all their interactions and if they don't see the value in forging a true partnership with their boards—then they're going to struggle to adapt and adjust to post-pandemic realities. The world has changed, and if they don't understand what being CEO entails, they will cling to their misperceptions and have difficulty learning new skills and adjusting their approaches.

I've emphasized the importance of authenticity and humility in this book as crucial attributes for today's CEOs, and these qualities are especially valuable in a digital environment. Prior to the pandemic, most CEOs could convey these two qualities in face-to-face encounters. They'd walk into a direct report's office, sit down a few feet away from them, and through words, tone of voice, expression, and gesture, demonstrate that they were being genuine and humble. It's much more difficult to exhibit humility and authenticity during a Zoom call. It takes time and practice to figure out how to do so, and CEOs who recognize that this is an emerging hidden truth—that they need to adjust their approach to achieve goals that were much easier to achieve in person—will benefit greatly.

CEOs CAN HANDLE THE TRUTHS

Who would ever want to be CEO after reading this book? I trust that a lot of candidates are up for the challenge, but I also understand that in a way, I've pulled back the curtain on this particular job. Too often, writers emphasize the glamour and power that comes with the position—it seems like being CEO is all about private jets, first-class accommodations, staff support, and rubbing elbows with the powerful and accomplished. Certainly there's some of that, but I've chosen to focus on the job's other realities—realities that many leaders may not grasp or that are the focus of criticism from observers who don't understand the CEO role.

The recent ESPN documentary *The Last Dance* provides a behind-the-scenes look at the last championship of the Chicago Bulls, and it reveals a lot of the hidden truths behind how teams achieve greatness. At times, it's not pretty. It's not just the glory of making the winning shot but the endless hours of individual practice, the challenge of managing often difficult team dynamics, and the hard work of sustaining excellence that allows athletes to have a winning season.

In the same way, this book doesn't focus on the outcome as much as the process. Everyone has seen the public face of CEOs, but this is about the private struggles and demands that often escape notice. My goal in revealing these issues isn't to diminish the role of the CEO but to help leaders understand what they need to know and do to succeed in the role.

The coming months and years aren't going to be easy for CEOs. Investors are going to be less patient. Management cycle time will be reduced. Talent will be less abundant. Add the need for greater speed and digital leadership to the mix.

You need to be prepared for all this if you aspire to be a CEO. One of our hidden truths is about arriving prepared, but all the truths in a way are about preparing for a highly challenging job. I realize I've offered a lot of ideas about how to put these truths into practice, and you should pick and choose. Every CEO faces a bespoke challenge. Therefore, experiment with the suggestions—use some, ignore others. Find the hidden truths that are most relevant to your situation, and focus on the learnings from those particular ones.

Finally, and perhaps most importantly, I hope this book provokes honest and open discussion about what being CEO is all about. For too long, this has been a topic discussed primarily on a surface level. People talk a lot about what constitutes great CEOs in terms of leadership qualities and successful strategies, but they don't dig down to the nitty-gritty of the job and the knowledge and actions that help CEOs be highly effective.

I once suggested to the former leaders of Harvard Business School to host 50 leading CEOs to participate in candid discussions about their jobs. As part of the program, I said we needed to guarantee participants that no media or recording devices would be allowed—"what happens in HBS would stay at HBS." The idea would be that these leaders could share the reality of their leadership journey and have an open and supportive dialogue about the challenges and the frustration of their roles. They could open up about the disparity between the public portrayals of the CEO with the day-to-day reality of the role. The Davos conference started out this way but has grown commercially and such that it is now entirely more style than substance. This idea was about creating an anti-Davos, one where CEOs could speak their minds and learn from one another and take guidance from each other and know that what they have experienced is the norm, not the exception.

For a number of reasons, this gathering has yet to get off the ground, but I hope this book achieves a part of that same goal and reveals truths about being a CEO that have remained hidden for too long.

Index